*In Quest of a Ministry*

# In Quest
# of a Ministry

## JULIAN PRICE LOVE

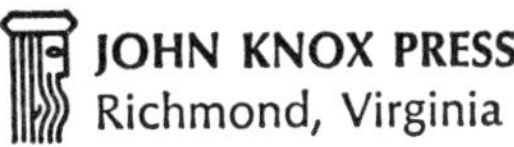

**JOHN KNOX PRESS**
Richmond, Virginia

Standard Book Number: 8042-1696-7
Library of Congress Catalog Card Number: 69-12369
© M. E. Bratcher 1969
Printed in the United States of America

To all those
who have been
my students and my friends
in the ministry

# FOREWORD

Some years ago I preached a sermon on the subject "How Preachers Get That Way." With his usual good taste and depth of perception, Dr. Love has given this theme a better title and produced a book to elaborate it with specifics drawn from his exceptional career of nearly half a century of teaching in two theological seminaries.

One of the stronger motivations for writing such a book was the valid "conviction that the great majority of church people still know little of what students for the ministry are like or what seminary life does or does not do for them." The author resists the temptation of a retired professor merely to recite reminiscenses of the classroom and the campus. Rather, he makes theological education live and glow through a series of sixty "vignettes" of former students fascinatingly classified under fourteen categories, ranging from "Men to the Manner Born" to "Failures," from "Bruised Reeds" to "Closed Minds."

A book on such a subject could hardly achieve its purpose without five of the characteristics of the author's fulfillment of his teaching vocation. One was the amount of time and attention given to counseling with individual students outside the classroom. A second was the consistent practice of inviting all his students in manageable groups to the hospitable home of Dr.

and Mrs. Love for social occasions which revealed facets of student personality divorced from classroom discipline. A third was the practice of visiting students in their various forms and places of fieldwork ministry while in seminary. Still another was the voluminous correspondence and frequent visits with alumni during the years following their graduation from seminary. Perhaps crucial to the accuracy of facts and the significance of judgments was the habit of jotting down in a cumulative file his reflections on the development of particular students at various stages in their careers.

Wherever he is or has been, Dr. Love is always the teacher. And if some former students should be able to identify themselves, despite his care to keep them anonymous in this book, they will find the author still earnestly engaged in teaching them.

Nor is this teaching confined to his former students. Much of it is directed to the rank and file church members who, in so many cases, do not know how to understand those who seek to serve them in the varied forms of the gospel ministry today.

Dr. Love looks back over a half century of theological education not merely to describe what has been. In a closing chapter he takes a prophetic look at "The Ministry of Tomorrow," seeking to evaluate some of its assets and pointing up some of its actual or potential liabilities.

The reader of this volume will gain an enriched vision of the diversity of ministers. He will perceive the error of a widespread assumption that the theological seminary is designed to produce standardized pulpit parrots. He will be moved as I was to give thanks that so many generations of ministerial candidates have had the privilege of exposure to the mind and spirit of such a teacher as Julian Price Love.

Frank H. Caldwell

# Contents

# AFTER FIFTY YEARS

No one can come to the end of a long period of teaching youth without a profound sense of gratitude. Nearly half a century in the classrooms of two theological seminaries has buried most of my early critical attitudes and disappointments and has vivified the sense of rare privilege.

Certainly there have been ups and downs. There were times when trying to get men to think for themselves seemed futile enough to tempt me just to pass out masses of my own conclusions, though fully aware that this was not teaching. There have been days when all effort put forth seemed to backfire, hours when even the fine fellowship of faculty appeared to evaporate like a morning mist, and times when rancor and distrust crept like a stealthy robber through my soul. I can remember one black hour when I thought I had decided that seminary teaching was not for me, at least not in the day or environment in which I lived; I wrote out my resignation and (fortunately) stuck it in a pigeonhole of my desk.

But all such reactions have been temporary and untypical. The passion to teach has overcome all the rebelliousness caused by the occasional animosity of students or fellow professors or by the harassing limitations of library, endowment fund, or misunderstandings by the public. And especially has it ridden herd on the inabilities and ignorance I kept finding in myself. The dominant note of this long experience has been joy. If I had my life to relive, I would want it to be once more mainly among students for the ministry such as I have known and in close fellowship with the churches which they and I have sought to serve. I can think of no one I know who, in the same sort of work year in and year out, has been so fortunate as I. For practically all of these years I have had just what I wanted to teach. For most of them there have been classes large enough to be inspiring yet small enough to permit the close individual contacts that make teaching live. During all of this time companionships with students and fellow teachers have made life radiant.

The position of the seminary professor has not, of course, always been safe. I gave up the pastorate of a particular parish in a day when a business friend could write me a stinging rebuke because at such an early age I had "left the firing line for a retired spot." But that same friend some years later encouraged me to "stick to this post in the front-line trenches." Seminary professors have become increasingly suspect as have all supposed intellectuals. They have been repeatedly attacked for putting this or that radical notion into the heads of students (most of which the students came loaded with), and they have been chastized for all sorts of peculiarities from doctrinal heresy to bizarre social theory. Yet through it all there has been an ever-increasing host of loyal and understanding friends who have championed both the right and the duty of the seminary teacher to lead his students in real quest for truth. And there has always been a steady stream of churches to call upon the ministry of the professor in pulpit, hospital, and ecclesiastical court so that he has had no trouble keeping alive to the needs of the local congregation.

And now, "What shall I render to the Lord for all his benefits toward me?" (Ps. 116:12, k.j.v.). It has seemed that it might be good to expose to the light of public scrutiny the characters and lives of students representing these four dozen years of ministry. Such a procedure is made possible by the habit I developed early of making notes of my impressions of students and modifying them from time to time as the men have developed or as I have seen new light. It is made inviting by the conviction that the great majority of church people still know little of what students for the ministry are like or what seminary life does or does not do for them. It has been made compelling by the hope that glimpses of ministers in the making, often with sequels from their later lives, will prove to be both a healthy experience and an enlightening look at the needs of the church of our day.

The desire to do such a thing has accumulated drive from two sources. For one thing, it has always been the practice of my wife and myself to seek the companionship of each student and of the wives of those who are married as often as possible in our home—at least once a year. While such a contact does not go as far as one could wish, it often sheds a light on a young life that neither the classroom nor the office can provide. Again, it has been our custom through the years to try to keep close through at least occasional correspondence with as many as possible after they have left the seminary. At present I can recall particular men with whom I have been in recent contact in forty-six of our fifty states and in some twenty-one foreign countries. This then is an adventure into the years of the building of the ecumenical church. I have rejoiced alike in students from north, south, east, and west, from Europe and Asia, from South America and Africa. At least a dozen times I have been favored with second generation students, and I came close to teaching one of the third generation.

Such an undertaking meets obvious difficulties. How shall I be true to my understanding of a given student and paint a word picture of him in anything other than realistic terms? And isn't realism always dangerous, especially when portraying to a somewhat uninformed clientele the inner being of those whom they have traditionally placed on some kind of pedestal? Won't such pictures, even though carefully drawn, have to reveal hidden factors in men's lives that should not be known by the general public? Couldn't they do more harm than good by displaying early traits of character and boyish patterns of behavior which have been outgrown in the course of the years?

I have sought to overcome these obstacles in several ways. The names given the students here memorialized are, of course, fictitious. While I believe all the sketches I have made to be true to life, I have deliberately modified nonessentials enough to make recognition generally impossible. I have carefully examined my files to discover the many instances in which students of varying temperaments have shown similar characteristics, and I have sometimes combined their qualities in the picture of the most attractive, the most outstanding, or the most representative of the group. And because, like all teachers from Moses on down, I have tended to idealize my own students, especially when I presented them before the Lord, I will be found to have over-shadowed many of these with the halo of some specially re-vealing moment. Does this mar a genuine picture? I think not, for often the portrait of what one is at his best is truer to the inner man than any number of snapshots of his thought and behavior in unguarded hours. Unadorned reality of fact may be less revealing than sympathetic idealization.

Let me confess that I have had my favorites. What teacher has not? Jesus himself had his inner circle. To spend oneself in the effort to bring out the good he sees in a person is of necessity to pass judgment on him. And since all of us teachers are very human ourselves, it is no wonder that we highlight men whose response to our efforts has been most enthusiastic. Not that we are taken in by those who adroitly court us. Despite the common student fear of being accused of polishing the big red apple, there is no greater error in rating an experienced teacher than supposing he is easily duped by such fawning. It is not at all hard to discern between the student who tries deliberately to cultivate his professor's goodwill and that other who natively responds to counseling and leading. The teacher's favorites are most often those who are quite unconscious of their role. And of course every teacher with even a few years' experience is repeatedly blessed by letters from former students who express some deep and often novel cause for gratitude which they never could offer face to face. But whether they have expressed thanks or not, I have been grateful for my students—almost without exception.

This gratitude is all the more remarkable when one realizes that seminary professors rarely have the privilege of choosing those whom they teach. We have to take what is sent us by the churches and make the best we can of them. If families, even of outstanding Christians, encourage their "brains" to go into business or science or other professions and are content to see third- or fourth-raters enter the ministry of their churches, there is little that the theological school can do about it. Oh, we can invite the higher-grade college student to our campus for a visit, and we can preach in churches on the need of quality as well as quantity in the ministry, but if this falls on deaf ears of parents or college professors or even (God help us!) of pastors, we are doomed to mediocrity from the start. Yet the results of the seminary's careful cultivation of even second-rate men are often nothing short of amazing.

The method of these pages is not to present lengthy biographies, but to draw a series of vignettes highlighting types of men. I have never ceased to marvel at the variety of those who feel called into the ministry. Yet in the background of these pen pictures there will occasionally appear something more than the portraiture of individuals. Especially in the sketches of some of the later sections, one can trace the main theological, philosophical, and moral shades of emphasis that have successively held the stage during the years of my teaching; it would be useless, even if it were desirable, to try to remove generations of students from the environment that nurtured them. Prevailing methods of biblical interpretation, of various ethical and social ideals, of unchanged yet ever changing doctrinal systems have firmly gripped the more malleable minds of imaginative youth.

There is nothing surer in school life than that the current interest will change. What is wildly hailed as almost the final word by students of one day will have little meaning five years later. I have seen men excited over the question of getting churches to pay money into a common treasury out of which ministers' salaries may be apportioned according to need—size of family, cost of living, etc.—rather than letting one congregation be known as a $5,000 and another as a $10,000 church; and I have seen their failure to influence the church courts reflected in the total indifference of the next student generation. Before the Second World War the passion for studying social issues was enormous and quite widespread over many subjects. Professors were besieged with petitions for seminars and non-credit colloquiums on questions of militarism, alcohol, etc. But after the war, interest in any social concern could not be created, even with a skillfully directed discussion group; the religious faith of the individual was all the rage. It was the rise of the issue of civil rights that redirected a new student generation to lines where action as well as thought became vital, though the springing up of the various schools of the new morality played an important part. Then arose the strange phenomenon, blindly followed by many faculty as well as students, of stressing out of all proportion some dire social need and completely bypassing another issue just as important that had failed to ignite the public interest. Thus there has flourished a zealous study of the use and misuse of sex, while the old interest in the effect of liquor on the lives of men has aroused concern chiefly as the treatment of a disease, not as a moral issue. The seminary student, like the church which he reflects, gets to the boiling point on this or that question, only to lay it aside half studied for another that has come front stage. Thus the compassion that has pressed home the need for civil rights, for fair housing, for the elimination of needless poverty may well go the way of other passing concerns. We almost never stay with a particular problem long enough to develop and hold a concerted Christian point of view toward its solution. Again and again, like the Seer's church at Ephesus, we have lost our first love (Rev. 2:4).

These shifting emphases have betokened some sort of unhealthiness in the character of the seminary student. Sometimes they have revealed his retreat from life. He has not wanted to face some problem of his own, or he is pricked by the realization of his indifference to some human need, and he takes refuge in a new theological stance. His ardent pursuit of some writer who is hard to understand may often be a cover for his unwillingness to study his own heart which is still more baffling.

Times also run wild with change over the theological issues themselves. I have taught through the long, bitter fights over fundamentalism and modernism (both silly words) and have seen men honored or damned as they got branded with the label of conservative or liberal (both good terms). This type of theological strain passed, at least for a time, and there were born the successive stresses on the neo-orthodox, the existential, and such attempts at modernizing the gospel as demythologizing. In turn during my day of teaching I have had students who fell under the hypnotic spell of a Neibuhr, Rauschenbusch, Fosdick, Barth, Brunner, Bultmann, Kierkegaard, Cullmann, Tillich, Bonhoeffer, or whom have you! There are always idols in the theological marketplace.

Yet changes in style of belief and creed often tumble on the scene as unaccountably as do changes in dress. Now faculty and students go in for the daintiest and most beautiful of thought expressions; again they revel in the disorderly, the illogical, and the plain absurd. In some periods the interest of students in any problem—theological, moral, social—seems only an armchair affair, while at other times real involvement in the affairs of men is openly experienced. Of course students and professors alike get misunderstood at either end of the line. In the one case they are sneered at as living with their heads in the clouds and being without genuine interest in people; in the other, they are feared with alarm as those who meddle in things of which they have no real knowledge. No wonder ministerial students, like Paul's Greek audiences, seem all the time to be seeking "some new thing" (Acts 17:21, k.j.v.).

Seminaries themselves are subject to the changefulness of the times. When there is great financial prosperity, they tend to build for a big student influx that does not come. When the remorsefulness that follows such a debacle as the Second World War drives men to their knees, the schools of the church are suddenly bombarded by hordes of students for whom they do not have adequate facilities. In the one case, the seminaries vie with each other for students as the colleges used to do and sometimes stoop to disgraceful recruitment methods. In the other, they raise some new artificial standards, such as psychological tests that have gone beyond the reasonable to the bizarre, an undue worship of the highest I.Q., or an extreme stress on the college rank of an entering student so that the poor fellow finds himself in the midst of a mad race for grades in order to maintain his place. The forming of the American Association of Theological Schools has helped to lessen such tensions between seminaries, but it has not yet been able to settle some leading points of conflict.

I have seen the day when all graduates were herded toward vacant pastorates, whether or not they would make good shepherds of souls, since the ministry to the local parish is usually the greatest of all full-time Christian services. I have seen, on the other hand, the time when more and more students seek to avoid the pastorate for teaching or for administrative responsibilities and when the local church is counted by some to be passing from the scene. I have lived through the period when getting people into some congregation was the grand ideal, and when the building of finer sanctuaries of worship or more commodious units of teaching was the goal of the church. On the other hand, I have come upon the time when the local church seemed no longer of such importance—the "secular city" wouldn't enter it no matter how well equipped—so institutions such as coffee houses for communication between religiously and secularly minded folk came to be extension centers of the church along city thoroughfares, just as preaching in the fields instead of in the cathedrals became Wesley's method of bridging the gap 200 years ago. I have seen the day when the sermon was at the center of all church worship, its length not nearly so important as its thoroughness. And I have witnessed the change in the direction of group participation; the "enrichment of worship" with many old and new liturgical forms; the reduction of the sermon to a ten-minute statement of some thesis of the Christian life, often some bit of self-evident and innocuous chitchat. I have seen the time of the seminary's emphasis on group devotional life—the chapel service of the entire student body and faculty, the worship periods of student classes or dormitory sections, the study of how to pray. I have witnessed, on the contrary, the revival of a new intellectualism, largely separated from worship, in which the chapel period is thought of as an occasion for bringing big names to the campus and when attendance varies all the way from the casual few to the full house according as the speaker of the day is reported to be trite and dry or exciting and novel.

These years have also witnessed many changes in the economic condition of students. Not so long ago men were supposed to live sacrificially if they were called to enter the ministry; the ill-heated classrooms and the hard-mattressed sleeping quarters were counted on to engender something of piety that self-denial supposedly brings. But the seminary's competition for better students has brought air-conditioned efficiency apartments with the latest installed equipment, regardless of the fact that the student could not expect to live in such luxury after he graduated. The dormitories of modern theological institutions are a slap in the face of him who had nowhere to lay his head. I have also lived through the day when seminaries virtually forbade their men to marry, when the student couple was looked down upon as a semi-disgraceful curiosity to whom the church's Board of Education denied financial aid because of their untimely haste in starting a family. I have returned to the campus after a single year's sabbatical leave to see baby carriages standing in the seminary quadrangle and the unmarried man mourning his minority status. I have seen times when students expected to work hard to make their way and other times when they looked to scholarship aid as their due. In the seminary, as in "The Great Society," one faces the difficulty of helping people who really need help without rendering them or their fellows permanently dependent.

Times have changed too in classroom procedures. I have taught under a curriculum composed of many short courses, all required, and I have served with a condensed offering of fifty percent electives. I have heard men stress the minimum necessities of each department, but I have also witnessed the rise in favor of group seminars and free research. I have seen men regimented to particular courses by carefully kept attendance rolls and the jealous guarding of irreducible requirements, whether in biblical languages, church polity, or basic doctrine. But again I have taught in a day of growing indifference to regular lectures or classroom discussion so long as men read on their own and can pass final examinations—a testimony to growing European influence in our educational systems.

I have taught in situations where seminaries paid so little attention to their offerings that the schedule looked like a smorgasbord menu. And I have experienced the passion for self-study so intense that night followed night as the faculty sweated over one detailed revision after another until nerves became ragged and it was all but impossible to teach in any form. Perhaps the balance will be struck when seminaries come to realize that the genuine teacher can make good use of almost any arrangement of subject matter as long as he has freedom to be himself under God and be a fellow worker with his brethren.

But lest this seem to chronicle a day of shifting currents only, let it be proclaimed aloud that in all these experiences of changing and changing back there has always been an undercurrent of genuine stability. It is the appreciation of this by the great majority of those who enter the ordained ministry of the church that makes them different and yet the same as other Christians, that enables them to feel a call that is specific and yet no more real than the call of the Christian layman to be a banker or a farmer, a scientist or a housewife. This continual paradox of the ministry has never lost its significance and has made it possible to pursue the art of preparing men for it with fullness of joy. How often I have found in later years that students were more affected by their days in seminary than I would have guessed at the time. How often they have cherished memories, small though these sometimes are, that have influenced decisive moves in their lives. How often the real conversion of the man has taken place after he has gotten on the field and has found in the wear and tear of experience his deepest call. In the years of nearly half a century that I have watched men come and go, there have been only a few who have run from their problems. Many more have stayed with them until they found some sort of partial solution, even some crowning note of satisfaction, the fulfillment of hope in love.

It is tempting at the time of retirement for men to feel "after us the deluge." And indeed today's rapid shifts in point of view concerning seminary work do raise a fear and trembling and a relieved sense that "perhaps I got out just in time." It may be that an entirely different kind of seminary professor is called for in this new era, and that in the wake of the ecumenical movement an utterly new institution is invading the scene of the old denominational seminary. Yet, as I turn in the gathering twilight to dream once more of those who have been my students, I thank God and take courage.

# CLASSIFICATION

Any attempt to arrange one's students in groups falls prey to one of several errors: It ignores too readily the chronological sequence which has much to do with the making of types of men, it complicates the issue by distinguishing too finely between dominant character traits, or it oversimplifies the whole picture. Nevertheless, some sort of classification that does not too easily betray identity seems desirable. Many men could without straining be put into more than one category, but the attempt here is to arrange selected students in a way that will emphasize the most important qualities of their lives.

Men to the manner born are those who from the outset seem to have been naturals in the ministry. There are others who have been tested and made strong—men who without question belong in the ministry, but who had to pass through a period of adjustment. A joy to record is a selection of those who have been surprises—men who in their student days raised many different kinds of questions as to their suitability but who turned out well.

On the other hand, this series of vignettes, if it would be true to fact, must record the attitudes and actions of some who have proved in one way or another to be unsatisfactory in the ministry. There are those whom we include under the designation "bright bud; half flower"—men whose promise was high but whose fulfillment seems generally to be lacking. There are others who have been out-and-out disappointments—men whose early days looked as bright as those of the preceding group but who have left largely negative impressions wherever they have gone. There are a few who can be called nothing short of failures in either character or ability or both.

But not all men who go from seminary into the active ministry can be placed in simple categories. Circumstances as varied as life itself enter the picture. There are those whose life has been subject to limitations where family relations enter in. Others seem fitted for just one type of service and have been useful in special ministries. Still others can be best understood when we view them as contrasts to some of their own generation. Some are "bruised reeds"—men who have passed through one form or another of mental anguish but who have risen above their difficulties.

Two diametrically opposed classes of men in today's ministry are those with closed minds who know all the answers to begin with and seldom learn anything new and those who are rebels against church or society, men whose inquiring spirit leads them into extremes of experimenting with theological ideas or ethical practices and sometimes makes them arrogantly independent.

Most needing to be understood and backed by the church are the "martyrs of today's arena"—men who suffer for conscience' sake and often are driven from their places of service because of their convictions on this or that social issue or religious question.

This study of types of ministry concludes with a brief testimony from the personal side, emphasizing the relationship between ordained and lay ministry in today's world.

# Men to the
# Manner Born

---

## BEN

Hearty, wholesome, with a smile that was broad and true, Ben was not simply the hale fellow well met, but a man of deep and abiding goodwill.

He had come through his personal battles and had won them. He had not left behind him issues unclosed nor fundamentals of life unsettled. He had the virtue of deciding each problem as he went along. Even when he was young there was about him an air of finality and arrival; you always knew he was dependable. Before he married he took careful stock of his resources and worked out two budgets, one for ordinary years and one for emergencies. And he lived quite closely within them, in both kinds of experience, without becoming niggardly toward his family.

Ben had real breadth of interest. He read widely and discriminately, though not as deeply as one could have wished. He was always abreast of current events and concerned himself with their meaning. He had a genius for detail without getting lost in it, and this was a good part of the secret of his mastery in each situation that arose. He talked a good deal, but he always knew whereof he spoke.

Ben's was no purist mind. He knew the ways of the world.

He had been in an army camp and had roughed it with the lowest of them. He had gone over the top and had heard the shrieks of the dying and had seen unmentionable sights. Yet he was sane, splendidly balanced, steady as a clock. He had feeling and was not ashamed to show it, but without undue demonstration.

His keenest interest was in people. He knew them and understood them. He delighted in analysis of character, and he would take folks apart and examine them piecemeal with all the ardor of a scientist in a laboratory. But he would put them together again with the zeal of a disciple. He has not moved often. He says of each pastorate, "I mean to stay until I see at least one concrete change for the better."

Ben has always loved to have friends and to be well thought of. He has had no hesitancy in seeking success and he delights to please. This sometimes leads him into his one great error, a sort of Jesuitical end-justifies-the-means attitude toward life. He was known to join an extreme rightist organization and just as extreme a leftist without any sense of contradiction because he always remained critical of both and tried from the inside to win the devotees of each to something better balanced. He enjoyed taunting his idealist friends with the admission that he was a pragmatist, and he was truly a master in his use with people of just what would work in their case. Yet he was at heart too much the idealist himself to be satisfied with pragmatism, and there have been times in his ministry when he has stood forth openly for the oppressed, as when the Negroes of his community were seeking better housing, and times when he has spoken sharply against some form of evil, as when he publicly criticized the Ku Klux Klan in an area where they were popular with church people.

Above all, Ben was sincere, a gentleman in all his ways, with a polish that was not veneer. His heart was as sound as his body and his head. Although his fine physique denied it, he had had a breakdown in his teens and had existed as a feverish skeleton for many weeks. He rarely spoke of this experience and then only with awe, but he left the impression of one who had early met the strong man in his soul and had conquered him. One who loved him might occasionally gain some glimpse into his inner being and see that his hardy development had been accompanied by a real moral struggle. While he abhorred pietism as not genuine and any of the retreat mechanisms as lacking virility, he displayed a Christian faith that was devout without being mystical. His kind really mans the church.

# DAVID

David was one of the sweetest spirits I have ever known—not sweet in a sugary way, certainly not effeminate, but lovely in a most manly manner.

He came to the seminary at great disadvantage. His early schooling had been inadequate, and he had no money to go further with elementals. He would probably not have been admitted except for his high native intelligence, his quiet perseverance, and his wonderful spirit. He could endure any amount of hard knocks without complaining. He could take constant kidding for his mistakes and enjoy it with the kidders. He always brought to class a little pocket dictionary, and if anyone used a word he did not know, he would look it up on the spot. He took advantage of every opportunity to improve himself. And great was the number of his opportunities, for everyone loved him and he was invited here and there to many churches and into many homes. People got more wholesome fun out of having him around than out of televised sports. Children would stop their games to be with him.

David could have grown into real potential for the pastorate of a swanky church; men with fewer gifts for such a life have come out of our classrooms and have succeeded there. But he always wanted to be identified with the small and needy field in some kind of home mission territory. He was the classic example of the biblical "servant" in modern dress. And he never grew weary of just being with everyday people and becoming guide and stay to their lives.

I visited him over a weekend in a parish in the midst of the wheat fields. He asked me to preach for him that Sunday, but I told him I had come especially to hear him in his own pulpit. "Well," he responded slowly, with his fetching smile, "let's both preach; these folks can take it." And both preach we did—two full-length sermons in the same service. I still remember his text: "But Peter followed him afar off" (Matt. 26:58, K.J.V.). And I could never forget the comment of one of his members to whom I afterward spoke of the high quality of his message: "Oh, yes," she said, "but we didn't need it. We couldn't follow *very* far off, for he follows so close." Blessings on you, David! Your name should be legion!

# TED

More and more in the ministry of the American church, we find ourselves making exchanges with the business world. A few men leave the ministry to go into some form of business where they have discovered they can serve humanity better. Most of these I have observed have taken their Christian ideals with them into the business world where it is a real challenge to put them into use. But much more often, especially since the Second World War, the church gets men who have started their workaday experience in business and who, for one reason or another, feel dissatisfied and seek a less competitive field of life. Because they have known firsthand what men go through who face the dog-eat-dog attitudes of the world five days out of every seven, these men often make some of the most outstanding and sympathetic of pastors.

Such a man was Ted. Endued by nature with a preciseness of mind and habit, he had business training which had developed this quality to the full. He was thorough in everything he did, patient and careful with all he undertook. He was splendidly self-disciplined and he seldom allowed himself any sort of rec- reation until he had completed his agenda of work for all departments. Moreover, his experience in the business world had necessitated frequent public presentation of ideas and programs, and to make himself most effective in these appearances he had taken a great deal of training in vocal expression. This of course stood him in fine stead when he entered the ministry. If he sometimes preached from the pulpit or spoke in private conversation with an overly exact tone and with labored clarity, at least it was never said of him, as it is said of so many ministers, We can't hear him. Again and again people have asked me, "Why don't you teach your young men to speak out so that they can be understood?" I have long held that the chief difficulty in hearing men lies in sheer laziness on their part, that if they will only take the trouble to project their voices, most of them can be heard by all but the very deaf. I know there are exceptions, for some men simply do not have the voice box. Such men probably should never enter the ministry; the denial of a voice is a call to serve elsewhere. But most of them can, if they will, project their voices. Ted puts into his speech the same energy and careful practice that he puts into his preparation of materials. He has already worked everything up in a complete fashion before he lays it out in the presence of the individual or the congregation.

If prima donnas can spend hours practicing their scales, if great pianists must employ long portions of each day at the keyboard, certainly the man who has the message of God to give can afford to take time and thought with all he says. He is on a more important stage than that of the concert hall. And the gospel is artistry as well as plain message; it is to be made winsome as well as direct.

# ALFRED

Al was one of those wholesome, reliable, completely sincere men who give the lie to the belief that the youth of today are going topsy-turvy. He was truly humble without hav-

ing any idea that he was (isn't humility always unselfconscious?);
his ready response to each situation was positive and heartening.
He had to drive a long distance to the seminary each morning,
and he got home late at night. But he was always on time (except once when a giant snowstorm blocked the roads), and he
was wide awake and alert to every idea that was put forward.
He could do a great deal of work in a short time because he had
learned to concentrate. He was not afraid of new proposals—
whether in theology, critical studies, or ethics—yet he was no
easy mark for the faddists. He thought things out clearly and
accepted or rejected the new as carefully as he did the old.

Al went through seminary confident that his mission was to
serve overseas. The foreign mission agency of the church was
delighted with him. His wife also ranked high with them, but
because she did not have the amount of formal education which
their standards required, she and Al did not get the appointment.
I was shocked and feared the disappointment would floor him,
but he took it with his usual good spirit. He then turned down
invitations to some "good" fields and followed the beckoning of
a little home mission station in an out-of-the-way corner of the
Lord's vineyard. There he invested his fine Christian character
in the lives of those who are among the keenest judges of character in this country.

There was one thing that might have turned Al in another
direction. He really desired to win a fellowship on graduation,
and his academic record was high. But he was a member of an
exceptionally bright class, and by the time all the available
fellowships had been parceled out, Al was left the next man
in line if there had been but one more to award. This disappointment he also took in stride and said it would give him all
the better chance to dig in deep on the problems of his isolated
community. And here he served for years without seeking
advancement—probably not satisfied in the final sense, but content in the biblical meaning. He has met everything from riots
to the God-is-dead pessimism with the same steady assurance,
even as a giant oak weathers the storm and still stands straight
and tall. Bless you, Al, you put heart into all who know you!

# IVAN

Few of my students have had a splendid opportunity like Ivan's to mold a changing public opinion. The product of an unusual childhood, Ivan has been all the more careful of his influence to make the home the center of Christian experience. A ministry that has embraced pastorates at home and service abroad culminated at just the right moment in a choice between satisfaction with things as they were and a chance to influence the thinking of a large segment of the church toward greater realism in the work of the kingdom. And he chose the harder and more glorious way.

His has been the gift to make clear to many leaders that the church does not *have* mission but that it *is* mission. He has had the foresight, the careful planning, that has brought into joint consultation a significant selection of workers in fields abroad with key men and women of the church in our own country, so that for the first time many of them have understood each other and have really listened to different viewpoints. He has had the courage to face the new day when portions of the church overseas have become impatient with the role of dependents and have sought to express independent thought and action, even to the extent of throwing overboard most of their relations with the Western churches that first gave them life. He has had the faith that has led him to turn down other fields of service where his ten-talented mind might profitably have been used and to stick to this one area of activity long enough to make a lasting impression.

Stay with it, Ivan! One of the biggest mistakes in the ministry of the church has been our failure to follow clear through on the wider vision we have caught. Men's minds are not changed overnight. Long years will be needed to implement the radical transformation of the church into one worldwide body of Christ. We are still beset by the selfish gestures of those who whine their old tune, We gave the money to found churches abroad; we should determine what they do with it. Lead into the day when self-importance passes from the servant church!


# ALLEN

The race is not always to the swift nor effectiveness to the loud shouter. Allen was soft-spoken and did not strain for recognition. Yet in the student body, among the faculty, and in the churches where he has ministered, he has won the admiration and the love of all. After following his career closely for some years, I should say that there are at least three reasons for his becoming one of the most remarkable influences for good that we have ever sent into the ministry.

In the first place, Allen cultivates continually an unruffled depth of spiritual understanding. He has always been a real student, but he never shows off what he has learned. He waits for the appropriate moment and then with some clear, brief word he crystallizes everybody's thinking with something that has the ring of finality. Back of his study you can always feel the life of prayer and commitment, the kind of power that is never dogmatic but that expresses aptly his latent strength.

In the second place, he belongs to that generation of students who have stressed in their theology the cross of the Christian as well as the cross of Christ. Following the Second World War there was a revival of interest in the Savior's cross. In the mid 1950's this was heralded as the high-water mark of Christian thought. But frequently it became an escape mechanism. If "Jesus paid it all," there is not so much required of me. If salvation is entirely by grace, it doesn't really matter what I do. Of course this is the old problem of antinomianism that Paul contended with in the days of the establishment of the Christian faith on the frontiers of the Roman Empire. Thoroughly set against any form of legalism as he was, Paul was just as heartily opposed to the use of what Bonhoeffer in our day has called cheap grace. In his student days and in his ministry since, Allen has always made it crystal clear that trust in the saving power of the cross of Christ was incomplete without taking up one's own cross and following him. Nor has this been mere dogma with him; it has sprung from his own life. I have witnessed enough behind the scenes to know that Allen has often quietly sacrificed himself, has often brought into the framework of real cross-bearing some of the deep disappointments he has had, some of his repeated frustrations. He has never advertised his own heartaches, but he has learned from his use of them to bear the burdens of many. He has again and again exemplified the love that seeks not its own.

The third reason for Allen's lasting impression on those who know him springs logically, though not necessarily, from the first two. He has always stressed as chief among Christian doctrines the note of joy. He has diligently searched out the springs of rejoicing in godly people, beginning with biblical examples and coming on down to our own day. In times of cynicism and apathy he has met everyone with triumphant faith. He could never be called flashy; he is not the bombastic enthusiast. But the silent and pure streams that continually feed his life make the joy of the Lord his strength.

God grant us more men with this threefold combination: depth, crossbearing, joy!

# RALPH

Among those who are outstanding in faith and life there is always a smaller circle and in the long run usually just one whose life means everything to one who knows him. An entire mountain range may be awe inspiring, but generally a single peak stands out in solemn glory. With Jesus there were Peter, James, and John, and within even that group there was the disciple whom Jesus loved, whom the church has long identified with John. Such a one need not always be outstanding in every particular. John would probably not have compared well with some others of Jesus' band in eloquence of speech, organizational ability, or prophetic powers. But in spite of Paul's passionate struggles with the meaning of faith, it was John who became the deepest theologian of the early church, the one who understood such finalities as "God is spirit," "God is light," "God is love," "We love because he first loved us."

So it was with Ralph. He was a good student but not the best. He was an attractive person, but I have known those who were more immediately winning. He was a good churchman, though I have had pupils who have gone further in their service through ecclesiastical agencies. He was an excellent pastor, almost without a peer in this area of the ministry, always keeping in touch with those whom he had served in an hour of need, yet sometimes mistakenly reminding them years later of a time they had tried to forget. He was a most loyal friend, though he did not explore the depths of friendship with a wide variety of people.

There was something that drew me especially to him and held me there. I was years in discovering what it really was, but I think his secret lay in the fact that from the very beginning he understood love in the New Testament sense as a self-giving. Not that he would have formulated it so exactly. Even in later years he might not have given a satisfactory definition. But without studying it out, and by spiritual instinct, he interpreted it in life faultlessly.

In his student days this interpretation came to light only if one accidentally discovered what was done quite privately. If, for example, there was some student who was not fitting in well with his fellows, Ralph somehow managed to sense it in time to be a particular friend of that boy. If there was one who was not getting along well in his classes, Ralph made a point of studying with him in an offhand way as though he needed the fellowship in study as much as the one who was behind. If there was a fellow who was lonely or homesick (and even at the seminary level of education this happens more often than one might think), Ralph somehow managed to be a companion, not obtrusively but very naturally, so that his friendship was appreciated by the brilliant and the slow alike.

I think the greatest compliment I ever saw paid to a seminary student in all my years of teaching was made inadvertently to him. It happened when our school was entertaining delegates from eight or ten other institutions in a regional conference of the Inter-Seminary Movement. Ralph was made general chairman of the arrangements committee because everyone knew he would take the job seriously and oversee every detail without omission. When the conference was over (and it had been an exceptionally good one), a group of visitors, the unavoidable committee of thanks, expressed appreciation to the chairmen of all the subcommittees in turn; praised the housing and eating arrangements, the speakers by name, and all those who had even minor parts on the program; and completely forgot to mention Ralph who had been behind the scenes in it all. After adjournment, when they recognized their oversight, they were mortified beyond measure. But actually they had paid the highest recognition possible to a servant of the Lord who had been so inconspicuous and so self-effacing as to be forgotten.

Ralph's ministry after seminary days was always in the urban church and always in the midst of many people. He had an infinite capacity for knowing individuals of all ages and for sensing their special needs. He served in many youth camps and conferences and directed many a boy and girl into a happy and useful life. When the Second World War came, he considered long and prayerfully whether or not to become a chaplain, and he arrived at this unique conclusion: "I can do more good by staying with the church and the city field which these young fellows have had to leave, by comforting and sustaining their parents, and by keeping in close touch with them than I can by leaving this field I know so well in the hands of a stranger." And so faithfully did he fulfill this conscientious role that he would write as many as 200 letters a month to fellows in the armed forces, some of them youth who were not even in his own church but whom he had come to know in some conference and who were often being neglected by their own pastors. He would receive regularly thirty to sixty letters a month, so he told me, from men who came to call him the home front chaplain. He would spend hours writing answers to such questions as How can I help but hate those who are killing my buddies right by my side? How can I think of God as I see the ugliness of war? How can I fight the temptations of drinking, swearing, and passion when there is so much of it around me? He seemed on the verge once of taking a stand as a conscientious objector to the whole military procedure, but he never did. When asked about it, he would sadly shake his head and say, "The church has never given enough peacetime instruction to produce any large quantity of genuine C.O.'s."

Dear Ralph! You have had no easy life yourself. Sickness and the death of loved ones have repeatedly dogged your career. But through it all you have remained sweet spirited, gracious, unspoiled, wholesome, genuine to the core, and, above all—to me—my pupil who has become my teacher, my intimate friend in the Christian way. What you have been could hardly be better expressed than by one of those young soldiers who was early torn from home moorings: "His counsel was always backed by his life."

# Tested
## and Made Strong

## VERN

Throughout the years of my teaching I have again and again been disappointed keenly with the pulls that have drawn gifted men away from the church's ministry. Some such men consider carefully and even longingly the opportunities of lifetime service through the church and then turn to science, industry, or some other profession. The common explanation is that these fields seem to open up more readily to men of large abilities. Often the parents' pride is the catalytic agent in the case. I was especially shocked to have the mother of a bright youth with whom I was counseling and who was greatly interested in the ministry say to me, "Joe has too good a mind to spend it in the pulpit where mostly mediocre folks will hear him." And that mother was treasurer of her church's missionary society!

It may often be that such young men subconsciously know that their very gifts may easily become a handicap in a profession where humility of spirit is so essential. Yet we may be glad that the Master did not say it is impossible for a man of many resources to enter the kingdom, only that it is very difficult. There have been indeed relatively few seminary students in my experience who would rank among the top one percent of their college classes—not too many who in their childhood would have shown with the "Quiz Kids" or in their late teens and early twenties would have been selected for competition in "College Bowl." But there have been some.

Vern was one of these. He was the only child of a godly home. He came to his preparation for the ministry with strongly preconceived notions about the large field of influence that would be open to his talents. Like the early sun of a summer morning he blazed forth upon the faculty and his classmates with astounding light. In his first year he was very sure of himself; then questions began to rise within. He was not altogether orthodox in his beliefs; wouldn't this jeopardize his standing? He was given to rather extreme argumentativeness; hadn't this already proved a stumbling block to his acceptability among his fellows of milder speech? He was by nature rather cold and theoretical; wouldn't this work against his approach to people whether in the pastorate or the teaching side of the ministry? His evaluation of himself, while perhaps higher than justified, was fairly realistic, and he did not want to waste his life on a futile investment of mental energy where there would be no adequate return.

I remember well the crisis point in his decision. He had been scorned by some of his associates in a way that hurt deeply. I happened upon him when he was all wound up inside and ready to explode. And explode he did, for so long and in such intimate fashion that I dared not leave him until the storm had passed.

Vern finally found his place. After a couple of false starts he came to see life more in terms of the personal equation. He warmed toward people; and, aided by a most compatible wife, he has rendered service, especially to troubled youth, that has reflected both his own struggle and his God-inspired triumph. Had he followed his secondary bent—toward science—he might well have become engaged in some project of outer space or have developed in some laboratory a new solution for a problem of modern living. But he has harnessed top brain power to the service of the inner space of people's lives, and he is bound to be one who hears at the end his Lord's "Well done." There is no premium on ignorance or smallness in the ministry; to it there may well be brought the finest of heart and mind.

# SANDY

There are those who enter the ministry with little sense of sacrifice because it seems to be a natural for them. There are others who are quite conscious of a sacrifice because they have been running for years from the call and have only reluctantly yielded to the love that "wist to pursue." Sandy belongs in neither of these common categories but in a class by himself.

The spring before his entry into the seminary, he had still not determined to become a minister. He was a star athlete, graceful and supple in every physical movement, and the life of a coach held chief claim upon his interest. But during the summer following his graduation from college, he faced squarely the need as he saw it in the lives of many young people as well as the qualities of mind and heart with which he had been endowed to meet such needs. He said very little when he came to us even though he was friendly and talkative by nature. Yet anyone who cared could see the yeast working in the batches of his thought.

He dropped into the office one day and sat down with a sort of wondering expression on his face, for a while trying lamely to formulate in words something that was fomenting within him. "What's the matter with me, professor?" he blurted in bewilderment. "When I decided last summer to give up becoming a football coach and enter the ministry, I was quite ready to make all the sacrifices this would involve. I wasn't mournful about it, I didn't have any martyr feeling, I was willing to give up for Christ's sake all I had counted most dear, but I didn't really think I would be happy. Now I've been here two months, and I've never been so happy in all my life. What am I still lacking?"

What a delight it was to point out that his sacrifice was all the more Christlike because he found it joyful! How splendid to sense the flow of true happiness through his genuine enthusiasm! And he has kept it ever since. It has been my own joy to follow him closely in his ministry, to share fellowship with him on occasion in each of his several pastorates, and to see firsthand how his joy in life has been contagious for hundreds of his parishioners. Not that he closes his eyes to evil or makes little of hard problems or hides himself protectively in his own fine family. He has grown in the realism with which he has faced hardened people even as he has grown in depth of thought. But his expanding theology has never produced the rationalist, nor has his handling of mean situations tended to make him at all cynical. Always that sense of genuine joy is the first thing you note about him. Always he gives the lie to those who think the minister is out of touch with the world. He does not argue, for instance, against the death-of-God theology; he lives the joy of the Lord. He does not bewail the church's abstraction from the secular city; he ministers in a very secular city and makes his church a wholesome meeting place with the sacred. "What's the matter with me?" Nothing, my dear fellow. The fact that you enjoy all of your ministry, the sacrifice included, is your token of membership in the kingdom. The fact that you lead so many others to a life filled with joy, in a time when joyful emotion is not the order of the day, is the proof that you found your true place in the economy of God.

# ROLAND

Why in this "enlightened age" do some people still think that to enter the ministry is to escape all the temptations that other flesh is heir to? The minister is a real man—a more heroic man than many others—quite generally a man of higher standards and sounder ethics than most, but still a man subject to all the buffetings that can be experienced in this world.

Roland was a delightful fellow. No one would ever have

thought of him as having any serious problems. Yet behind his frequent boyishness and his happy smile it was not too difficult to detect, when he was not on guard, a kind of lonely sadness. I wondered about it a good deal but was not ready for the revelation when it came.

It was evening. I had been to a dinner somewhere and had stopped by my office on the way home. I heard on the second floor the voices of several men I knew well and thought I would take a minute to run up and say hello. Roland was among them, looking strangely unresponsive. After we had all chatted for a bit and the group had dispersed for their evening's work, he lingered on. "Would you," he asked rather timidly, "come into my room a little while? I've something I want desperately to get off my chest." Sensing the urgency, I put aside other plans for the evening and sat with him while he talked.

The upshot of a long, frank disclosure was this: "I know everybody thinks I'm a model young man, and as far as any outward break is concerned, I've never committed any. But I don't understand it. Sometimes there comes over me an almost irresistible impulse to throw everything to the winds—not only my ministry but my manhood. Sometimes I feel that I'd just like to go out and spend a whole night in complete riot and be just as bad as I could be. Maybe I'd just like to find what it's like; I don't know. But I'm afraid of something deeper and more violent."

I shall leave it to the reader to imagine the course of our conversation. My purpose is not to show how I saved a man from falling. In fact *I* didn't save him. God worked through the innate goodness of his years to keep him in the straight and narrow way. And he has made a splendid minister, helping many a needy person at the opportune moment and never giving anyone cause to feel that he had stepped aside from the path of righteousness.

My real aim in recording this experience with one of my favorites is to note concretely how deeply the tempter lays his wiles upon the human heart. There is a bit of bad psychology that persists in spite of its badness; it runs something like this:

Only those who have been really immoral, both inwardly and outwardly, know the power of temptation. You have to get down in the gutter to understand the depth of sin. Exactly the opposite is, however, the case. The tempter does not spend his sharpest attacks on those who fall readily; the easy prey does not know the real agony of temptation. But the more a man resists, as Roland had done, the more he feels the tug of the tempter who will not let him be. The purer the soul, the more truly it knows the depths of sin. And paradoxical though it sounds, the only One who ever experienced all "the fiery darts of the wicked" (Eph. 6:16, k.j.v.), and who ever understood the complete filthiness of sin, is the only One who never yielded to the tempter's devices—who "was in all points tempted like as we are, yet without sin" (Heb. 4:15, k.j.v.). In his name we bid all the Rolands to overcome.


# EMMET

Emmet was a fine mixture of brilliance and practical interests. He was always knee-deep in philosophy and was bitten by the bug of the realistic theologians. His own way of developing his thought was supremely important to him. On the other hand he was vitally concerned in the life of his fellow students. If he made case studies out of some of them, he could be easily forgiven, for his love of the men themselves was genuine. I was particularly impressed by him during one summer vacation. We had gone through a rather severe winter at the seminary—both in inclement weather outdoors and in a rather nasty spitfire of argumentativeness inside. Heresy hunting was in the air, for it is epidemic at times, and you simply have to live through the period until newer interests arise to choke it out.

Emmet wrote me from a rather idle summer in which he was recuperating from physical exhaustion and was getting in a lot of reading that he had laid up for such a time. He was, however, living in the vicinity of a conference grounds and was at least partly aware of what was going on there in the church's training of youth leaders. His letter mostly concerned these college students and, in addition, a seminary classmate of his who had received rather rough treatment in the church courts where he had seemingly been batted around from pillar to post.

"You know," Emmet wrote, in words which I paraphrase, "while I was in seminary I did not love everything that went on. And now that I am out I am even more suspicious of what I fear was going on behind the scenes. At least Dr. X seems to have followed Charley wherever he has sought to go and has taken out on him his prejudice because Charley would always side against him and champion the thought of other members of the faculty. Now I admit that I think Charley is confused, but who isn't these days? If he may be counted as one of the problem children of the seminary, why doesn't the old school at least follow him with sympathy and guidance rather than with distrust and heckling? Is this just the seminary's way of getting rid of a product it could not prevent but doesn't care to own? If this is the case, I wonder whether it wouldn't be better if the disease could be cured at its roots. If there is anything in the gospel record of our Lord's following the wayward sheep and seeking to win it back to the fold, I wonder why that approach has not been taken with Charley. And how much of the school's attitude is represented in this conference going on in my home town? Here you have literally to wade through the slush of professional cordiality and superficial hilarity. There is a prevailing complacency in the attitude of the teachers of youth here which bothers me no end when I consider the impotence of the church in this, my home state. The instruction being offered these youth is of the conventional, unrealistic type. Here we have a civilization cracking up about our very ears and our traditional culture is being challenged. The totalitarian nature of our religious faith needs to be explicated, if ever, against the totalitarian demands of the world. Yet here our most promising youth are led through a dreary, ethical commentary study of Genesis. The great appeal of the realistic theologians to me lies in their attempt to construct a relevant system on the basis of concrete situations. Yet

here I see the same abstraction that I tilted against while in
seminary."

Well, neither situation was actually as bad as Emmet thought.
In part he was disturbed by his own enforced idleness. At least
some members of the seminary faculty had sought to follow
Charley through his various torturing experiences and to help
him as far as he could be helped. There were at least a couple
of live leaders at the youth conference who dealt in more than
abstract generalities. Nevertheless, Emmet had struck a note
that must be sounded wide and clear. No true shepherding
institution can be satisfied with its success as long as even one of
its flock who has any of the qualities of sheephood is lost in the
wilderness mazes of the world. Realism is not the end-all of
being, but without it the most hard-working seminary must
confess its failure to be the true fold.

# Surprises

---

## ERNEST

Out of a modern Ur of the Chaldees he came to us, not knowing where he was going. With a wife and several kids (he never called them anything else), trusting to get a job with which to support his family (and he got it), trusting to be able to care for his family all the time he was in school (and he never let them suffer), trusting he could sail through the three years in a solvent condition (and he graduated without owing any man a penny), trusting to be able to take a course for which he was not academically prepared (and he finished with honor), trusting that he could get along in a social environment that was strange to him and his (and he won lifelong friends there), trusting to be able to stand up with men who were his superiors in physique and culture (and he never was stepped on), trusting to be able to serve satisfactorily the church that he had scarcely known in his youth (and he became both a successful pastor and a sought-after member of the boards and agencies of his denomination), trusting to be able to hold his own with men of dignity and advanced training (and they loved him though he remained rather crude in manner and used colloquialisms freely). Trusting! That was his secret—trusting, not with a blind

ignorance, but with the understanding of an Abrahamic commitment. And such trust won.

Only once during his three years with us did I see him really
cast down, and then largely because he thought that the seminary he had come to cherish had been unfair in one of its choices
of men. Almost always he was buoyant and optimistic. "This
will come out all right, professor. Don't worry about me." Though
he would occasionally talk about his difficulties, he would always
end up by stressing how much more he had to be thankful for
than most of the other fellows. His wife was a demure some-
body but a peach of a manager (she had to be!). Together they
brought up their boys and girls, gave them a good time, taught
them to work hard while they were enjoying life. Ernest worked
hard himself day and night and seemed always to thrive on it.
His unfailing wit crackled on the needed occasion. His sense
of gratitude was spontaneous: "Oh, don't you know it's great to
be alive and have the privileges I've got."

Dear fellow! You'll never be famous, but you'll always be an
inspiration to those who know you. You have never abused your
native histrionic gifts. Your humility has ever led you to acknowl-
edge your faults, yes, to be the first to discover them. Your open-
mindedness has kept you learning new ideas and new ways while
at the same time you have tested all things and held fast the
tried and true. After some years in the ministry you seem
fresher than ever in the good sense of that word. You apparently
have found the fountain of youth that others have long sought.

I can never forget one moment. I had a couple of hours between trains in the town of your earliest pastorate. I called
you and you took me joyfully over your little parish. And before
I left you asked me, not with sanctimoniousness (you were
entirely free of that, thank God!), but with your natural spon-
taneity and piety, to do one thing for you: kneel down with you
in your little clapboard-walled study and consecrate it anew
with prayer. I have no recollection of the words I uttered there,
but seldom has the spirit of a time of worship remained with me
so clearly through the years. In that spirit I pray now, God bless
you and make you a blessing, even as he promised Abraham.

# FRANK

The boys called Frank a city slicker, and his pastorates have all been in cities. "Because he's so handsome," sneered one who was somewhat jealous of him. But strange as it may seem, there are actually in my experience very few good-looking men in the ministry, and still fewer who succeed. Their good looks prove to be their downfall or at least get in the way of their being real ministers. Or is this just sour grapes on my part?

At any rate Frank was the exception: handsome and a real minister. He was by nature as pleasant as the smoothest politician, yet he did not use this gift for getting ahead. He served people graciously most of the time, but he could be critical and sharp and very stubborn when he thought someone was badly in the wrong. He was an excellent preacher, endowed both with clear thought and ready expression. He has served conscientiously, if not brilliantly, in the courts of the church where conscientious rather than brilliant service is needed.

Being in city churches, Frank's ministry has always been subject to the efforts of special interests to control it. He has been under pressure from extreme rightist groups most of his days. He has seldom if ever yielded, yet he has kept the admiration of most of them. People always say, with a wave of the hand, "Oh, Frank has a way with him," and they suppose that explains his keeping even keel. But his successful handling of situations goes deeper than that. On one occasion, when he was called upon to head a committee dealing with the case of a fellow minister who was under fire, he succeeded in getting a verdict that not only denounced the persecution of his brother in no uncertain terms, requiring restitution as well, but also announced a decision limiting the minister to more considerate ways of working. The trouble that some men in public life seem to attract to themselves is seldom simple to analyze. Even when they are obviously the butt of ill treatment, it is generally in part the fault of their own tendency to set the chip on their shoulder and invite others to knock it off.

But it is Frank's relation to the seminary that I have been particularly interested in following. So often men who go far in the echelons of the church forget "the quarry from which [they] were digged" (Isa. 51:1, r.s.v.). But Frank has been among the most loyal of alumni, not just in showing interest and in securing contributions from the well-to-do of his constituents, but in actual labor for the seminary in spite of a schedule crowded most unmercifully. I asked him once what his keenest recollections of seminary days might be, and he replied, "I knew no professors in the traditional sense, but many friends who bore the title and the intellectual abilities of professors." Small wonder that from Frank's pastorates others have gone to study for the ordained ministry of the church!

# DALE

Here is the saga of a man who was our student for one year only and whose life was cut short in the making. Dale was among the least prepossessing of our entering class that year. He was timid to the point of being scared in the presence of even a small group of people, quiet to the point of being exasperating when anyone desired to draw him out, and unsocial in his demeanor until you wondered whether he lived entirely within himself.

At the end of the year he was nervously considering summer work. One of the faculty, more daring than I would have been, recommended that he go under the Home Mission Board to the mountains to work among the lumberjacks. If any man seemed unsuited for such a strenuous assignment, surely it was Dale. Most of us shook our heads and said that he wouldn't last a month, that he would be out of his element and would panic.

But he stayed with it until a week before the time to return to school. We had heard nothing from him, for he corresponded with no one, faculty or fellow student. The Board had as yet sent us no report of his activity. Then it came—the news trickling through that Dale had been out with the lumbermen, that a great tree was being cut down, that he slipped awkwardly into its path and had been instantly killed.

This was only the beginning of a long series of reports. In the early summer the coarse lumbermen had scorned and ridiculed his presence among them. He had seemed to be from another sphere, some unreal place beyond the workaday world. His Sunday services had been attended by only a handful. Only a few men had any acquaintance with him at all. But gradually his influence had made itself felt. The same men who had come to the common board in the beginning of the season full of their loud guffawing and their shady stories had begun to quiet down as they took their place at meals. Dale did not even attempt to offer grace publicly, but bravely he had quietly bowed his head each time and had had his own word of thanksgiving which they could feel even though they heard nothing. And amazingly, so the word came to us, every man in camp had gotten to remaining silent at the table until Dale lifted his head —something quite unusual for a group of hearty, hungry outdoor workmen with the rough instincts prompted by the absence of wives and sweethearts. Dale had never gone around to their bunks calling on them in the evening, but had sat quietly in their presence at their camp fires. He had stood and watched them at their work during the day, never correcting them when they let out oaths or got into fights, seldom having more than a word to say. Apparently he had not counted for much of anything, yet after his tragic death man after man came through with his testimony that Dale's life and example had made him, in part at least, a different man.

What shall we say to these things? Was it largely the accidental death that had glorified Dale in their eyes? Or are the framers of ministerial criteria missing something when they insist that every man who enters the ministry should be an extrovert, that only the socially dominant can play successfully the minister's role? That Spirit who works when and where and how he pleases has used more than one such as Dale to change more lives in his stumbling silences than others have affected by being hale and hearty fellows well met. God does work in many a mysterious way his wonders to perform. Who are we to limit him?

# LUTHER

Cute, witty little man! As sharp as a tack, with a precision of speech that sometimes made one writhe, and with a two-edged sword in his tongue that could cut to the quick and that never failed to divide between joints and marrow. You never were just certain what he meant, but you were uncomfortably conscious of the fact that he had thought deeper on the subject under discussion than you had. His comments were often devastating in their finality, sometimes cuttingly sarcastic; yet when he wanted to, he could be perfectly enigmatical. He was particularly clever at reducing the abstract to the concrete, hard problems to simple proportions, seemingly endless discussions to quick decisions. And there were times when he delighted to confound you with some absurdly light conclusion to a heavy premise.

He seemed on the surface to have little conscience. He could say the most daredevil things with a straight face. Yet underneath he was always true to his ideals. He appeared oblivious to feeling, and only those who knew him best ever saw him on the verge of tears. You felt that he scorned the effect of circumstances; yet if this page could record all it might, it would chronicle the astounding mystery of his deep and poignant pain, his sufferings of soul at wrongs heaped on a brother, his exquisite grace of sympathy.

He was hard to know—not only to get acquainted with, but to fathom once you got acquainted. He had himself learned life unnaturally, had come through a love of books to a love of men; and he retained a certain artificiality about all his ways. Yet he was a philosopher, deep and worthwhile, and in the quiet interior of his soul he had met the bogies of life and unmasked them. To one who knew him and who had a fellow feeling, he would display upon occasion a keen understanding of the issues of life. He was a parable on two feet, even as Mark's Gospel describes a parable: blinding to those who had eyes to see and saw not, simple and convincing to those who had spiritual understanding.

In what a surprising way I miss him now that he is far removed! I find myself now and again wishing that I had learned what he meant by this or that cryptic remark, that I could sit down and talk over with him some of the most personal things I shrank from mentioning when we were together. The challenging thrust of some one of his proverbial sayings often focuses itself in light upon some dark corner of meaning, a quick white light that reveals and yet leaves me wondering just what has been uncovered. When I come to comprehend him, I shall have entered the kingdom.

# WILBUR

Candidates for the ministry in the "regular line churches" come today from all sorts of unexpected backgrounds. It is often remarked, for instance, that now a smaller percent pass through the church-related college and more come from the university. What is not so often realized is that some of them— some of the best of them—come from the small sects.

This was true of Wilbur. His parents were both participants in a group that stresses speaking with tongues and the manifestation of the gift of the Holy Spirit in forms that many of us would feel are mere vagaries. He grew up dissatisfied with this expression of religion, yet with deep faith. Often when a man makes a transfer from some overly enthusiastic cult to a more orthodox type of religion, he has a violent upset and comes denouncing his upbringing. Not so with Wilbur. He never lost his affection for his parents or made fun of their religion. When I went to preach his ordination sermon in our own church, he saw to it that his folks not only were invited but were given places of prominence.

Wilbur became a quiet and thoughtful servant of his field. Gifted with the ability to talk to many kinds of people and to persuade those who are hard to win, especially attractive to young people, he has majored in the work of youth camps and conferences, yet in such a way as never to lose the regard of those of a more emotional strain among whom he was raised. He wrote me once, "I have found that the more we put into life, the more we get out of it." For most people this is no new discovery, but for Wilbur, who had been brought up to think overmuch of what he would get out of his religion in the way of special blessings, the steady giving of himself in unheralded ways has brought a fresh vision of the meaning of life. Our "main line churches" may need to reconsider what we owe to some of those whose faith seems crude to us. We may need also to have some of their visible emotion—even their bombastic joy—passed through the crucible of our politer forms.

# KEITH

It may seem strange that a seminary professor would contend strongly for a student with a low I.Q., especially such a seminary professor as I was—always urging higher academic standards and tougher admission policies. Keith came into the seminary under a very lenient policy; indeed he was clearly an exception. His I.Q. was dangerously low, right on the edge of the figure that the experts consider an impossible score for a minister. We were induced to take him because he came from a good college and had a fair record. So we gave him the benefit of the doubt, especially since the I.Q. scores are not, like computers, deities with absolute omniscience. We required him to do a retake a little later, and again he rated very low. Yet he did acceptable work in all his classes except those that called for abstract thinking. Here Keith had to take the elementary work more than once, and questions were raised as to whether we should advise him to continue.

But I was not the only one who fought for Keith. His splendid personality and fine Christian character had impressed many of the faculty as well as laymen in a number of churches. But of special consideration was the fact that, more than many of our brilliant students, he had the gift we all look for: he applied himself with every ounce of ability he had. If some of the men who have passed through my courses had worked half as hard as Keith, they would have set the world on fire. Yet he never seemed to be driving himself. The reason was clear: Keith was excellently motivated. He really knew why he was in the ministry; he really cared to serve; he really wanted to be able to lead a congregation. And motivation won the day.

More than this, Keith's work was seldom ordinary in the sense of lacking imagination. He not only put himself into whatever he was doing, but he delighted all those who worked with him. This was true of the carpentry jobs he took to help put himself through school; it was true of the work he did on student committees. Everyone enjoyed serving with him and especially under him. He and his wife lived in our home one summer while we were away, and not only did they take splendid care of it (all the students we have ever had live any time in our home have done that), but Keith thought of so many little things to do that added to the attractiveness of the place. There was always some kind of plus to every act of his from driving the couple next door to the hospital in an emergency to a rather novel twist to his term paper.

Keith loved people and could talk for an hour at a time with a merchant about his wares, a farmer about his fields, a machinist about his shop, a housewife about her chores. Somehow he kept his ear close enough to the ground that he seemed always to know something firsthand about the problems of each of these, even though he was without experience in their lines of life. He was by nature expert at listening and feeling.

I do not hold that the mistakes made by some denominations

during the frontier days in setting impossibly high standards for their ministers' education have bearing today. The church of almost any area of our country includes schoolteachers, scientists, business executives, who know the score of modern living better than the average minister. I am committed to the belief that our academic standards should be high today if we do not want to shame the gospel by inept handling in the presence of a cultured generation. I am not swayed by the argument that this man, though ill-prepared and rather stupid, will do in some backwoods community; this is part of the reason that we have backwoods communities. But I do want to give a chance to the man who knows where he is going and uses every ability he has to get there. Keith finished in the lower third of his class, and he cheerfully took four years to complete a three-year course. But he has done a real work in the ministry. He has kept up a slow reading of good books. He has helped one church really grow, and he has formed one new one. I.Q.'s are important, and certainly we must never play fast and loose with them. But *motivation* is above all determinative for the minister's role.

# HARRY

I have always been prejudiced against transfer students. They have generally been running away from some defeat that they ought to face right where they met it. Frequently it has been a failure in some academic department where they have not liked the professor and they think they can come through better in another school. Sometimes it has been a case of social misfit, and they want to start over with a clean slate. Occasionally it is the proximity of the second seminary to the college a certain wonderful girl is attending, but the very nearness is apt to be a drawback to the academic record of them both. More often it is the theological viewpoint of his first seminary which the student has found uncongenial, and he flies to an unknown where he hopes he will feel more at home. In most of these cases the transfer student finds it difficult to equate the work he has had with any offerings of his second-choice school, and the dean of this school is apt to be as confused as the student in determining what credits to allow. As a result, the man seldom finds the change to his satisfaction and he rarely does even as well as he had in the school from which he came.

But there are exceptions. Not only was Harry the one that proved the rule, but he brought new life and light from his early experience. He just hadn't liked the big Eastern complex from which he came. His professors had been steeped in Barthianism, and to Harry the work of Barth, necessary perhaps as an antidote to the European situation, was only a sour note in the symphony of humanity. To be sure, he had read very little of Barth himself; he had gotten him largely in the classroom secondhand. He had no acquaintance whatever with the newer emphases Barth had come to make. But he did stir up a lively discussion among some unthinking traditionalists of our Midwestern locales. In fact his rather boisterous denunciations of Barth did more to set some of our students reading this twentieth-century Calvin than all the urgings of their doctrinal professors had been able to prompt.

Moreover, Harry had had an unusually interesting piece of fieldwork with rather broad connections. He had been in a group of students who had organized noon shop meetings among workingmen, and he transferred with him to our setting both enthusiasm and know-how for such service. He was a skilled musician on several instruments. He had native ability to stir new interests in rather indifferent men. The result was a sizable group of fellows whom he led in a type of voluntary reaching out for men that was not colored by the compensation they received from church-oriented occupations.

For a time I feared that Harry's zeal would run away with him and his buddies. But he turned out to be well balanced. The same men he was leading in unregulated student ministries got him absorbed in theological and social emphases that were new to him. He came for the first time to see the relation between creed and conduct, between worship and service.

Perhaps there is a suggestion here of the possibilities that lie in interchange of students between American seminaries. We send men abroad for a semester or an entire year of their ministerial training so that they may get a greater variety in their approach to religious leadership. But the climate of institutions varies from coast to coast in America almost as much as from the United States to Europe. We find nearly every sort of theological, ethical, social, and economic creed represented at one point or another on our continent. And still our men tend to get set in one atmosphere of thinking and to feel out of the swim when they move into another. The broadening out into the more ecumenical church may well begin in our own land. Interplay of faiths, of denominations, of sections of the country among the seminaries may serve to expand and deepen the ministry in the name of him whose kingdom is from sea to sea.

# Bright Bud; Half Flower

## FRED

Fred came to seminary with one of the most impressive personalities a school could wish to see and with a correspondingly fine academic record. His was a clean, open face—handsome without being a target for sentimental oh's and ah's from the feminine gallery—and he won a ready way into the hearts of all. Conscientious in his work, relishing research, willing to take any responsibility and see it through, he was put at the head of any list of recommendations we were called upon to make. Impervious to flattery, he continued to learn as if he knew only a little, and he wove each new bit of that learning into the pattern of the fine endowment with which he had begun.

Inevitably Fred won a fellowship and just as inevitably he went to a large university to use it. Here a strange metamorphosis took place. While doing his graduate work, he used his spare time to help the representative of his denomination on the campus. He literally lived at the church house and drew many youth there. The change that came over him was hard to understand and still harder to express. Without yielding his faith he came to overlay it with much of the doubt and sneer of the university life around him. Without actually compromising his high standard of ethics he identified himself with all the most modern thinking about free sex. Without drinking liquor himself he began to scorn the idea of its being harmful. Without overtly insulting his past friends and bosom companions he overlooked them in a condescending way.

Even harder to follow in the change that came over Fred were his constant references to problems in his life. Like anyone else he had had his concerns in his undergraduate days, but they had never seemed to bother him unduly, nor did he tend to magnify them. But now everything became a problem to be solved, and he felt the solution to be farther and farther in the future and one that might never be found even by a man who sought the hardest. This came to be the chief meaning of life for Fred; he was one of those who reveled in the quest and who cared little for the find. He delighted in books and ideas that were exciting; indeed if a thought had no offer of thrill in it, for Fred it was not worth following through.

But most difficult of all to accept was Fred's sudden marriage to a girl he had known only a few months. She was everything he had not been: careless in appearance, unfriendly, homely, an intellectual to whom the spiritual seemed almost meaningless. Yet Fred was devoted to her, and they seemed to get along without a break.

Fred became a staff worker in a large metropolitan church, but he has seemed never to arrive. Outwardly faithful to his task, he became deadened in zeal about everything except hunting a solution to the problems of the universe. He apparently was understood from the first by a small inner circle of his new associates, and he unquestionably felt he had found the way to communicate with the men of his time. But even many of those who followed his ministry shook their heads and wondered just what he meant by this or that.

Perhaps even yet, in some divine intervention, the true purpose of Fred's life will become clear. Those who have known him long and well love him even when he passes them by without a second thought. Someone's love, in the New Testament sense of self-giving, may yet pierce the barrier, for this kind of love is the one real answer to Fred's problems.

# ARTHUR

Art was poor as the proverbial church mouse. He came to the seminary with exactly fifty cents in his pocket and with nothing anywhere else. For that matter, he had no foreseeable source of income except such as student scholarships might provide or a small field of service offer in compensation. Yet he stuck it out and never let it be known that he sometimes went hungry.

Of course many would say that his want was largely his own fault. He took too literally Jesus' command to give to those in need and to do it without questioning. I have known him to come back late at night from a village church he had been supplying, give the last nickel in his pocket to the beggar at the bus depot, and walk to the seminary, bag in hand, though it took him an hour to climb the hill. A fool? Undoubtedly but there are many kinds of folly, and the fool for Christ's sake is often hard to distinguish from the fool for his own sake.

I became interested in Art's home and community background and received this discerning bit of correspondence from a former teacher of his who had known him long and well: "Arthur is very poor, and along with it has little money sense. He is extremely generous, and of course rarely gets to show it financially. He has what seems on the surface a kind of irresponsibility, but this is from a true sense of values, really, rather than from thoughtlessness. He is well liked by everybody, but lets everybody waste his time. He is very tolerant and understanding of others, but we are looking to you to help him find an inner discipline."

And I never did. What was the reason for my failure? I tried, but the whole idea of discipline was as foreign to his practice as was meanness. Like Topsy he had "jes' growed," and the concept of a life inwardly controlled was miles beyond him. Counsel to be reasonable with the use of his time and means meant absolutely nothing to him. He would let any fellow student come in his room and waste his time with meaningless jabber even when he was trying to finish an overdue report.

It was not that he resented our advice; he never understood us, for we never learned to talk his language of simple faith and love. After he got out of seminary, he treated his meager salary in the same way as the study time he needed to guard each morning. There are ministers who fail because they refuse to be interrupted in the quiet of their study for anything short of a death. But Arthur was always among people. He walked everywhere, saying it was good for him. And the people he befriended let him think so.

Poor fellow! Or should I say, infinitely rich fellow! Always happy, always content, always looking on the bright side. I have often wondered how long he could have kept it up, especially with a growing family, but he died young and I can only guess what might have been the outcome in the long run. Yet the question haunts me still: Are some men actually called to be fools for Christ's sake in just such ways? Or, more arresting still, are we all?

# STEWART

Not all the problems of seminary students have to do with how they shall think theologically or how they shall operate a parish. Some are concerned with apparently mundane matters like social adjustments and thoughtfulness toward people's feelings. Just as the finest church worship service can be spoiled by the janitor's failure to have the air in the sanctuary freshened, so the most able minister may ruin his influence by carelessness in dress, habit, or notice of some parishioner's kindness. I was once asked by the faculty to tell a certain top-notch student that he simply must wash the back of his neck and wear clean shirts. Fortunately, in spite of a reputation for grumpiness, this particular fellow complied graciously.

But the case that almost floored me was that of Stewart. He was a thoughtful young man but one of the absentminded kind who seems even in your presence to be miles away. During the summer following his first year with us he went up into the mountains to serve some very needy folks. He reported in the fall that he had enjoyed his work and had gotten along well with the people. The new term was well under way when I received a pathetic letter from a woman in the region he had served. She had gotten my name from someone and had written me with real Christian diffidence. I refrain from quoting her letter, even with corrected language and spelling, but its gist was this. She had felt the young seminarian seemed lonely and perhaps a bit homesick. The choicest products of her garden were not ripe before he left, but a week or so later she had put up several jars of fruits and jellies and had sent them to him at the seminary. She had waited a month but had had no reply. Now she was writing me, not to have me worry him about it ("the box wasn't worth that much"), but simply to ask if I would find out in a roundabout way whether it had reached him safely.

I meditated on this letter until the fire burned. I could see a dear little old Scotch-Irish mother of the hills slaving away over her hot stove, putting up jar after jar with loving thought, getting it packed as best she could, and making it up the creek to the post office carrying the package on her lap as she rode her horse. I could see her now wistfully wondering whether her labor of love had been useless. I hastened over to Stewart's room and found him in.

"Did you," I asked, "in your summer up in the mountains make the acquaintance of a Mrs. X?"

"Oh, yes," came the instant reply, "she was one of the most faithful members of my congregation." And he added, "She was a mighty good cook."

By this time my ire was rising higher than I realized. "Since you've been back have you heard from her?" I asked.

"Yes," he responded with a sense of appreciation, "she wrote me a real nice letter about the work of the summer. It's hard for her to write as she had no schooling."

"And did she at any time since you've been back," I persisted, "send you a box of goodies?"

"Why, yes," he answered slowly, apparently becoming suspicious for the first time, "she sent me some of her canned fruits and jellies and other things."

"Have you ever tasted any of these?" I continued in my self-assigned cross-examination.

"Sure," he smiled, "the fellows on this floor and I have already eaten everything in the box, and they were all good too."

"And have you," I concluded the interrogation, biting my tongue to bide my time, "have you written to thank the dear lady for her pains and to tell her how good her things tasted?"

"Why, no," he replied absently, "I don't believe I have."

The pot boiled over at this point. It would scarcely do to print the tongue-lashing with which I lit in on that fellow. When I finished I thought he might literally throw me out of his room, but he seemed genuinely repentant and he promised me he would write her that very day. His repentance must have been genuine, for he has made his way with people since in spite of occasional reports of thoughtlessness or absentmindedness, and he has risen to a position of some trust. It may be that my extreme righteous indignation was for once the thing that was most needed, even if it spent itself on what seemed to be a small matter. "Take us the foxes, the little foxes, that spoil the vines . . ."(Song of Sol. 2:15, K.J.V.).

# DOUGLASS

It was always a question when Doug was serious. He was so full of fun and jest that even his closest associates were unsure at a given moment whether he meant what he said. He could tease most unmercifully, and he carried out his propensity even with the most solemn of his friends and parishioners. In fact I have at times shuddered lest he be taken with real offense. Not that he ever meant any, for he has always been at heart kind and gracious. But he would make puns in season and out; the fellows used to say he would joke at his grandmother's funeral.

This characteristic has of course stood him in good stead with that type of person who likes to be joshed. Moreover it has done some real good in limbering up the outlook of some of the long-faced folk who feel called in any congregation to identify piety with solemnity. I am confident that Doug has been a real godsend to some of those who have mistaken a liver complaint for Christian character.

But there is a limit to all things, and the limit to continual joking comes early. Doug has never had the close contact with people in deep trouble that others of my students have experienced. It is not that he cannot be serious. He has at times shown himself capable of the finest appreciation of a trying situation in the life of some hard-pressed soul. But people aren't just quite sure, and all too often they turn to someone else when the trying moments of life are on them. Doug himself was a sort of hothouse product in a protected home, and the question is natural, Does he know the deep hurts, the serious problems of people concerning the identity of self, the depths of uncertainty in so many souls?

Doug can preside at a state occasion with real dignity. No matter what the theme of the gathering, he is always "nice" and agreeable even when he obviously doesn't agree. But you never know when he is going to think it proper to introduce some horseplay. In him the monkey and the saint live together, and for those who realize that the combination is sincere he is a real find. He reads good books, sometimes heavy books, but he is as apt to caricature a Niebuhr, Brunner, or Tillich as one of his buddies. He actually thinks deeply on current issues, but he often treats them so lightly in public that people feel he doesn't care.

For those fond of seeking Aristotle's golden mean there is no satisfaction to be found in Doug. He can no more leave off seeing the funny side of a serious problem than he can fail to be a true friend. But be this said to those who feel he goes too far with a good quality: he has never been without calls to strong churches, and his popularity in any given field remains. He is no fly-by-night. Evidently he meets a real need in the church spectrum of today, for most of us tend to take ourselves and even our world too seriously. Yet such a man plays a limited part in kingdom ministry.

# MALCOLM

In the nearly half century of my connection with theological seminaries one of the most constant problems has been the relation of the practical training of men to their classroom studies. I have always believed that training on the field should go hand in hand with study of the Bible and theology, of church history and the science of preaching, rather than come after the academic side was complete. In fact I pioneered in advocating the growth of the two together in days when such a relationship was unpopular in most seminaries.

This does not mean, however, that I have always been in favor of the current emphasis or of the technique employed. I have seen the time when fieldwork was looked upon as a necessary evil to give a man financial support while he was engaged in the all-important enterprise of the achievement of knowledge. I have even known seminary leaders who tried to keep some churches in their vicinity in a dependent condition so that they would be income-producing points for their students. I have again and again seen the home mission money of the church poured down a rat hole in the effort to keep alive a given preaching point for the seminarian. This has been criminal misuse of the church's funds.

Even when the practical training was thought of as something higher than a bread ticket, the fact that a man had fieldwork did not necessarily mean that he thereby was profiting educationally. Malcolm was a case in point. He was extremely unfortunate in his field assignments all through his seminary career. The church which he first served told him they knew they were guinea pigs for him to experiment upon. Another said they were so sick of seminary students that they were considering closing the church. Still another informed him that they would come listen to him preach but they didn't care to have him in their homes. What could a young man learn from such experiences? Certainly nothing that would encourage him to think of his ministry in large terms. More than one man has received the wrong impression of the church in his seminary days from the cheap excuse for churches he has been called upon to serve.

But there is a healthier side to the picture and one (thank God!) which is being photographed more and more. I rejoice that I have lived to see the day when at least to some extent the time spent on the field and the time spent in the classroom are not thought of as rivals. I rejoice that fieldwork is becoming field education, much more carefully integrated into the curriculum than heretofore. I rejoice that in many seminaries today field experience has careful supervision from pastors assigned to the job, pastors who meet with the field education director of the school and learn from him what is expected of them in training a young man as well as what they can hope to get out of the service he renders. Such procedures, like anything else that is improved in organization, can of course end up in much ado about very little, but I am convinced that not as many Malcolms are experiencing dire disappointments in this line during school days as once did. Many churches that are served by students are of course delighted to have them and have long thought of themselves as participating in the training program for young ministers. It is a cause for rejoicing that now theory and technique are becoming much better correlated. More power to the educative process in all its phases!

# Disappointments

## JIM

A homesick, self-centered boy was Jim. "How you all this mawnin'?" he would inquire with his Dixie drawl and his glowing smile, always trying to hide his native heartsickness.

There was something peculiar about that smile. It was cheery and catching, yet not what you would call bright. Back of it seemed to lie some hidden pain, and pain always appeared to be in that young life, especially the pain of a boy's healthy appetites unsatisfied—held down respectably indeed but not actually controlled. The smile was never revealing. In spite of his outward friendliness you never felt you knew him or what he was really thinking behind the mask of that pleasant face.

But his was a popular personality—always good-natured, never taking offense, refusing to quarrel or even argue over anything, avoiding almost with terror the trouble of taking sides. Friendly with those who were anything but friendly with each other, he would win at least a grudging allegiance from both the sophisticated and the unthinking.

Yet how he could impose on his many friends! He would smilingly admit he was lazy, indeed seemed even fond of being told so. He would take any amount of teasing with a way about him that would make most people enjoy serving him even when they scolded themselves for being so easily duped. He was built for comfort and often came to be ministered unto rather than to minister, with a way of getting around people that got them unconsciously to do the ministering. A slick politician, many said. He held in turn practically all the student body offices and later many important posts in the courts of the church.

Poor fellow! The Foreign Mission Board did well to question your none-too-ardent application in fulfillment of your pledge given at a summer youth conference. They were well advised when they asked you to do that hardest thing of all for you—make up your mind definitely first. No wonder they said, "Too uncertain in his thoughts and actions." What trick of fate was it that made it so hard for you to decide, that kept a church waiting until it grew too tired to call you as its pastor, that gave you good taste but left you the prey of passing fancy? What trick was it that led you repeatedly to respond to the insistence that the time had come for action with the silly answer, "Sho 'nuff?" You have often reminded me of Ruskin's "smiling image" that had to be "pushed from behind."

Men liked you and you have had ability to burn, but somehow you have burned much of it up to little purpose. Oh for stamina in that will when you use your fine talent for leading boys on a camping trip! Oh for more poise in that self-assurance with which you have so easily won at the tennis net, on the basketball floor, in the classroom, or in formal debate! Talent, yes—winning talent whenever the chips are down, a certain bet in any kind of contest. But, alas, an uncertain something when you must appear in your own strength alone without comparison with any others! Can it be that part of the revelation that awaits us in the next world is the understanding of such great promise and such limited fulfillment? Sho 'nuff?

# ALBERT

One of the hardest lessons for a seminarian to learn, or anyone else for that matter, is the use of time. The churches have been remiss in their training at this point. They have been so eager to get the funds into the treasury that they have limited their teaching of stewardship pretty largely to the use of money. To be sure, at young people's conferences the stewardship idea has often been extended to the use of talents and the dedication of life to the service of God. One might think that by inference this would be applied to the use of time, but even the smartest among us does not make quick carry-over from one avenue of living to another. It simply doesn't do to assume that the teaching of general principles is enough; these principles must be constantly brought down to the concrete if the Christian life is to be well rounded. It is not sufficient to convert a man and then say in effect, Now you find ways of using your faith in your life. Most people still need to be shown, not only The Way, but also special *ways*.

This is particularly true about the use of time. One of the wiliest snares of the tempter is to lure us into going through our days as though we had all the time we want to accomplish the job of living. Only as we get older and see companions of our youth dropping at our side, do we suddenly wake up to the fact that our time on earth is limited. The regular flow of day and night, the recurrence of the seasons, the opportunities that are constantly being renewed, lull even conscientious minds into the slumberland of wasted time. Learning to use time is part of the whole problem of mastering a self-control.

This is such a common ailment of student days that it is difficult to pick out any group of men, much less any one man, who has been a notable derelict in this regard. Yet I can never forget my incessant struggles with Al. Pleasing, popular, gifted with many talents, Albert could get out a piece of work in half the time it took the more pedestrian minds. Yet he simply could not get it done when due. He would dillydally and make all kinds of excuses to himself and to me. I found he did all his other professors the same way. When he finally got the work in, it would generally be good, though always showing that lack of finesse which an earlier start would have made possible. Al knew his fault and many were his tears and promises of repentance, but the change never came. He was as late with everything in the last term of his senior year as in his first semester of school. He flunked one course simply because a real emergency arose in the last week and he literally had no time to finish his work.

Al has had a good ministry in some respects. He has served faithfully and at times brilliantly and has been an inspiration to many people including students on college campuses. But he has never gone as far nor been as sought after as his potential would have suggested. He still leaves the finishing of his sermons for Saturday night, the calling on someone who has asked to see him until tomorrow. He is all too often tardy in meeting the counseling services scheduled for his own office. His excuse of being "so busy" is no doubt sincere in his thinking, but actually it covers up a constitutional defect.

In vain many of us have labored with men like Al to get their work in on time; in vain we have cut grades down as a penalty; in vain we have urged the gaining of the delightful experience of being able to review one's work before turning it in and so make real improvements. In vain also we have sought to spike the usually false notion, I do my best work under pressure. And in vain I have repeated again and again my favorite motto, "The only sure way of being *on* time is to be *ahead* of time." Time is simply not in the consciousness of youth!

There is of course a still deeper ditch into which the time waster often falls. He puts off dealing with some of the more definitely moral issues of his life. Al sometimes says he must "get around to looking up the old notes" someday to see whether this particular paragraph of an effective message is really his own or whether he borrowed it without giving credit. In many personal habits he is always "going to change this way of doing" but never does. He has, for example, given up cigarettes a dozen times, but he needs to face himself with the fact that he actually does not intend to write finis to this indulgence. He is going to come to grips "someday" with the question of whether or not he spends too much time on a given kind of recreation, but he fails to realize that his character has already pretty well solidified. Of course I am aware of the power of God to change men after many years of stalemate. The Holy Spirit works almost unbelievable conversions in adults as well as youth. But as time goes on, the likelihood of men giving him free rein to work decreases rapidly. And with ministers especially, as a rule the die is cast soon after ordination. "In the place where the tree falleth, there it shall be" (Eccl. 11:3, K.J.V.).

# EARL

Earl belongs to that fairly large number of men in the ministry who have tremendous drive. He has the ability to do a lot of big jobs at once and do them all well. He readily keeps details at his fingertips. He organizes his task to the nth degree without letting the organization ruin his spirit. He has tremendous ability to command the service of others and to channel that service flawlessly.

Earl is an excellent example of the need to fit the man to the field. Where a church is badly disorganized, where a parish has had little or no ministerial leadership, Earl has been an outstanding success. Where laymen have long been untrained and latent abilities have remained undiscovered, Earl has done a thorough job of enlisting the support of many different kinds of men and women. He has repeatedly gotten things going where stagnation had set in. His churches have become activistic.

Now if Earl had always been content to work in a parish which needed just such leadership, he would probably never have suffered a setback. But unfortunately he accepted a call to an already well-organized church where there was strong lay leadership. Here he seemed insensitive to the need of a change in his approach. He continued to begin at the beginning with people who were already far in advance. Soon he developed the reputation of being a dictator, of wanting everything done in his own way. Men as smart, talented, and well trained as he, who ought to have become bosom friends, were alienated to the point of restiveness and even scorn. I asked a fellow minister whether he thought Earl had lost his magic touch of success. His reply was, "I'm never concerned about Earl's succeeding; what I am concerned about is whether the church he serves will have any chance to succeed."

Only two possible paths look open to this type of man. Either he must examine himself so closely that he knows what kind of field needs his leadership and resolutely refuse to go to any other however strong and appealing, or he must learn that hard lesson for a go-getter of passing responsibility on to others. After all, the latter is what Christ did even with twelve rather stupid followers!

# LELAND

The formalist is ever with us. I confess I have never really understood him. The usual reasonings can hardly answer why any man who can think, feel, and speak for himself should hide behind a defense of secondhandedness.

To be sure, the minister ought to be dignified and utterly proper, at least when conducting public worship services or acting as a counselor in his capacity as a trained instructor. He must impress people with the fact that he has something they need. But this does not excuse an attitude that denies the priesthood of all believers and stresses the ministry as a position to be looked up to rather than a functional service.

Probing deeper, we are met by those who see in the sweep of church history a justification for parroting the words of an ancient creed or following the program of older ministers. Their reasoning is, It ties us in with the church of all ages. Yes, but the very words and methods being aped were given to the church by those who, as they were moved by the Spirit of God, spoke with originality and with an accent native to them. We will relate best to such giants of the past if we imitate not their verbiage, which may be terribly out of date, but their faith which lays hold of the mysteries of God. The fact that their language was sometimes beautiful may indeed justify our reading occasionally from them to our people, but no amount of appreciation of those who "put it so much better than I can" will ever atone for our failure to use the free gift of God within us.

Leland may once have been a man in his own right, but if so, he has long since forfeited that blessing. In private conversation he is pietistic and preachy. In public appearances he speaks largely in the words of others, always acknowledging his source to be sure, for he is scrupulous about legal honesty. His dress is always formal; his manner, reserved and distant. He has developed a singsong delivery far beyond that traditionally known as the preacher tone. When he reads prayers or declarations of forgiveness to his people, he rattles. I have heard him when the words were indeed lovely, but when the total effect was hardly different from what the reciting of the alphabet would have produced.

Leland says he believes in the enrichment of worship, something we all love to share. But richness and copycatism are not synonymous. One may indeed lead his people into the wealthy heritage of the church of all ages, but to be real to the people of today, these borrowings need first to flow through the personality of the man who uses them so that he does not appear in the role of a ventriloquist's dummy. To the people who know him and depend upon his service, no voice can so truly represent the divine as can the natural tones of their own minister, no words can so vividly declare the counsel of the Lord as those which their minister speaks in his own right, and no attitude or viewpoint can be so compelling as that which wells up spontaneously from the depths of his own soul while in firsthand fellowship with God.

# MAX

Jesus' parable praises the man of five talents because he used them to good advantage. The man with only one tends to become afraid he will lose it and so buries it in a safe place. But there are other men of five talents who try to use them all at once and who, in spite of frequent brilliant sallies into the spiritual markets of the world, become confused.

Such a case was Max's. Gifted along so many lines that one could hardly keep track of them, with a fine ability in all kinds of sports, a brilliant academic record in college and seminary, experience from childhood in a great variety of Christian enterprises, he seemed headed for grand achievements. But he never could decide which of his many talents to stress. Should he become a religious leader of youth in athletics? Here he could accomplish a rich ministry. Should he become a professional counselor in the modern sense? His ability to enter into the problems of people of all classes and to give them help in a non-directive fashion was apparent to all. Should he become a preacher of power and authority? His flair for the unusual approach, for an original handling of a subject, and his magnetic delivery combined to forecast a future that would make him a truly great pulpiteer. Should he stress the teaching element in his ministry, possibly becoming a professor in college or seminary but more likely hewing out new paths for religious seminars in the church at large?

Max could have become any of these with a leadership that would have been vital. The trouble was that no one man could become all of them. And he simply could not make up his brilliant mind which sort of man he wanted to be. So he temporized, always doing well what he did, being outstanding in this or that for a while, but never quite arriving. Restless and imaginative, he always saw greener fields elsewhere. May God grant that he shall yet be able to say of his lavish gifts, "This one thing I do." For of talents, as of money, it must be admitted, "How hardly shall they that have . . . enter" (Mark 10:23, k.j.v.).

# Failures

---

## ZEHN

Failure in the ministry sometimes is the fate of men who are good in themselves but do not fit the particular role the minister must play.

Zehn came to us with high recommendations. He was a model young man in character and disposition. He had served with distinction in the youth organization of his home church, in summer conferences and camps, and even in interdenominational groups. His college record was better than average, though both it and the psychological tests showed a decided leaning toward scientific subjects.

Zehn started well in seminary. He already possessed a good background in Bible, history, and philosophy. But as the course broadened, Zehn tended to an ever lessening degree of interest. In preaching and counseling he seemed strangely ill at ease. He became completely lost in the complicated problems of Christian education and in the use of even simple forms of church organization. To all our attempts to face his problem with him he gave polite but casual attention, and he was not at all communicative about his evident frustrations. He graduated rather far down in his class and left us with a vague feeling that we had somehow not quite reached him.

**For a year we heard little of him; then came the startling**

news that he was getting nowhere in his pastorate. Reluctantly he agreed to sit down with some of his former faculty and see if he could not come to a better self-understanding. Gradually the truth came out. We had thought he delighted in being the seventh generation of ordained ministers in his family, but it was the pressure of this responsibility that was troubling him most. As the only son in a family of girls he had been told repeatedly from early childhood that he must not let the family record be broken: at least one minister in each generation. He had striven valiantly to meet the expectations of townspeople and relatives. He had shunned any revelation of his true feelings to his teachers. He had put on an artificial happiness, carrying out what he thought was his duty. But there was an underlying note of bitterness in his response that we had not detected earlier. He simply had no natural bent for preaching, teaching, or church organization. He had come to the point where he knew that continued effort would only result in pretense.

Fortunately this experience of failure had a happy ending. Some of his faculty were now able to show him that there was no virtue in his keeping on with a work for which he had no real aptitude. Others managed with care and skill to disabuse the minds of his family and friends as to the glory in seven generations of ministers in one family. Zehn demitted the ministry without prejudice and started over again in a scientific course where his natural abilities soon restored his joy in living. He has carved out for himself a reasonably successful career. And he has remained active in the church where he renders an unspectacular but real service. Here was a "failure" caught in time.

# WALT

One of the most tantalizing questions in the training of today's seminary student is what to do about a psychiatric evaluation. Some would say that every candidate for the ministry should have one, and good arguments can be put forth for that stand. Others would limit the evaluation to those who show some emotional disturbance. Still others insist that such a requirement often does more harm than good by frightening the student who is not yet prepared to go to the psychiatrist as he would go to his family physician. Some even say that the disturbance is apt to be worse after such an experience unless it can be followed up by long weeks of treatment—a process which few men can afford. But I have often wished that I could get a reliable opinion of a given student from one who was both a first-rate psychiatrist and also a real Christian—not too easy a combination to find.

Perhaps my most extreme example will not seem too far-fetched to illustrate the need. Walt appeared odd from the first. He never was seen to smile. He worked for grades rather than for what he got from the subject. In his first year I think he despised me completely. Near the end of that year he came in to tell me that I had completely misjudged one of his papers and I would *have to* raise his grade on it. I tried quietly to explain where the paper seemed to be lacking, but he had worked himself into such a frothiness that he could not hear me. He even edged so near to me that he was standing practically on my feet emphasizing his demands. I was about to call for help when he finally backed away. Of course I did not raise his grade.

Later in his stay with us he turned right about-face and made me his confidant. He told me of the trouble he had had with his wife, of his many sleepless nights, of his unwillingness to serve under the guidance of a wise and patient pastor where he had been assigned for his field experience. He confessed to me one day (after a bit of probing on my part) that his mental and physical ailments were due in large part to the poison he had once taken in a suicide attempt. But he begged me to tell no one since he felt himself then to be on the upgrade and he did want to complete his work and atone for the past by going into the ministry.

I felt intuitively that he was still keeping something back. I found out the rest soon after in a most shocking way. I was working late in my office one afternoon when everyone else had left the building. He came in breathless, almost without knocking, and said he had to get it off his chest. He was a complete fraud, he had falsified his college credits, he had no degree from any school, he had forged the transfer papers that had come to our offices. I asked him what he expected to do, whether he would confess to the administration or simply drop out of school. "Neither," came the startling reply. "I'm on my way now down to the river to jump in, but I wanted someone to know the story after my body is discovered."

Now what do you do all alone in an office at six o'clock in the evening with a man who says you are the only one who is to know that he is about to end it all? I did what any other Christian would no doubt have done in such a corner; I sent up a spontaneous prayer for guidance. Quick as a flash came the consciousness that what was needed was to laugh this fellow out of it. Such a move did indeed seem dangerous, but so did any other I could think of. So I smiled and said with what outward composure I could muster, "Walt, I don't believe you. You haven't the courage to jump into the river. You've never faced anything in life with courage. I'm not a bit afraid of your committing suicide." We talked for another hour and he promised me he would try to get his life straightened out.

We did find that the credits were forged. He admitted at least part of the story to the seminary office and took his expulsion. Two or three of us tried to follow and help him, but he soon vanished from sight. I began to wonder if he really had made an end of himself, when he turned up one day in one of the sects, rather happily following their pattern with his wife and children. Explain such a man? You may have the job.

# MAURICE

If ever two diametrically opposed souls inhabited one body, if ever Dr. Jekyll and Mr. Hyde dissolved themselves into one another with hair-raising rapidity, they did so in Maurice. He was to me a character defying logical analysis, yet obvious in the main lines of thorough self-contradiction.

On the one hand, there was deep and genuine kindness, a gentleness and helpfulness that went out of its way to find a need and meet it, a generosity that was so unquestioning as to be often imposed upon. On the other hand, there was bitter and unrestrained hatred, malice that would blacken a man's reputation at the least turn of feeling, ingratitude that would make his resentment a weapon of annihilation against even a close companion. On the one hand, there was real delight in friendship, and he had a large capacity for friends. On the other, there was a lack of ability to be loyal to those friends, a sudden turning against them when it seemed unprofitable to support them any longer.

On the one hand, there was a love of truth and a fine ability to pick out the false and lay it aside. On the other, there was at times a baseness that knew no equal in anyone else I have ever known, a capacity to lie that was devilishly mean, a passion for insinuation that covered all its tracks with the avowal that he had been misunderstood, a trickiness that left no room for itself to be caught, a penchant for leaving a devastating impression of someone without actually saying anything at all about him.

On the one hand, there was a love of beauty and a delicate appreciation of art, a quickness to discern the effective from the merely showy even in the most modern painting or piece of music. On the other hand, there was a fondness for indelicate references that shocked and frightened a new and unsuspecting youth.

No one who knew him dared trust him. He could rip a man up the back with a sly thrust while fawning on him with his benign flattery. Yet many did not know and they trusted. They were blinded by his seeming grace. He attained large influence so that many a fellow student sold his soul before he knew and woke from a lulled drowsiness to pay with feverish breath the penalty of having yielded to the monsoon which he had thought was only a gentle breeze. He could command a tremendous personal following in almost any given church; was he not eloquent and convincing? Could he not "pull them in" with an evangelism that was church centered instead of kingdom centered? But he could also toss overboard his most loyal follower who had become useless to his self-centered purpose.

I know of no explanation of this man that does justice to any kind of psychology. He was not a hypocrite, though many thought him so; that would be too simple an analysis of his complex character. He was sincerely good when he was good and just as sincerely bad when he was bad. And he could change from the saint to the demon in the twinkling of an eye. I followed him to his room one day to congratulate him on his especially fine chapel meditation, only to hear behind the closed door his voice turned strangely strident, wildly berating some poor fellow for having discovered something about him he couldn't afford to have known.

That Power of control of which he often spoke wistfully had never taken possession of his life—the Power that cures the schizophrenic with a consistency of faith. That Power will judge him. Let no other dare!

# NATHAN

All seminaries that serve in this age of world conflict have the problem of the man who comes to study for the ministry mainly to escape the military draft. And all seminaries that I know anything about have been very conscientious in dealing with such men. It is understandable that those who at least verge on the position of conscientious objector find it difficult to analyze their own purposes clearly enough to determine whether they feel themselves genuinely called into the ministry of the church or whether they are seeking an out from a most distasteful experience. The government has long recognized the need for new religious leaders to be trained even during war, and it has not hesitated to exempt all those who are vouched for by their churches as bona fide students for the ministry. Many ministerial candidates today do not believe in this and will not accept such arbitrary exemption. But the fact that a man may be classified 4-D because of being in line for the ministry places a

great responsibility on church and seminary to know the sincerity of those under their guidance.

Our problem has been complicated still further by the fact
that some of us on the faculties of seminaries are ourselves conscientious objectors to military service and therefore have to be
particularly on our guard so we will not give easy credence to
the man who is hiding behind an exemption and is therefore not
really honest. So far as I know, all seminary professors, regardless of their stand on the military question, wish to honor and
support the genuine conscientious objector. As a matter of fact,
many of these boys have rendered creative service, some of them
as guinea pigs for the trying out of new remedies for dangerous
diseases, some as heroic rescuers of the wounded on the battle-
field to which they have gone out unarmed. But also, as far as
I know, there is not a man on any seminary faculty who would
want to support an *un*conscientious objector—to military service
or to anything else. No matter how much we would like to see
men freed from military involvement, no matter how incon-
sistent we feel a military draft to be in a democracy, we are
united in the stand that no man must be allowed to hide behind
a fake if he is to become a minister.

It did not take us long to find out that Nathan was of the
fake stripe. So we sent him away to discover his heart's true
conviction, for every man must learn to wrestle with his own
life. He never again sought to enter a seminary. If today someone says we robbed the church of a good minister, our ready
reply is that we do no robbing. Every soul determines his own
true standing before God. Our lives are "hid with Christ in God"
(Col. 3:3, K.J.V.).

# BILL

Many failures, especially those that get mired in
theological swamps, begin by tentative ventures on unfamiliar
ground.

Bill had grown up with a rather pietistic bent, and in his

early life he had been frightened from trying anything new. So when he came to the seminary and found himself free to venture out on untrod pathways of the mind, he at first drew back in shocked surprise and then by degrees grew fond of trying new ideas.

His first tentative efforts took him into the popular field of dialogue. Since he had learned that he must be ready to give a reason for the faith that was in him, what was more natural than to depend on his increasing ability to state logically the grounds of his beliefs? And since those grounds must be compared with the ways of the world, what could be better than to pit his wits against some of the ablest worldings? From this it was an easy step to questioning basic tenets of his Christian convictions until they became convictions no longer but trial positions which one might hold if he could establish a logical undergirding for them.

Soon Bill's passion was all for dialectic. Pitting one argument against another became his chief delight. The recognition that other ways of thinking might have as much validity as those with which he had been raised expanded into the feeling that no particular faith was really crucial. All systems of belief in all parts of the world were indeed only varied exponents of the human search for God. Beginning on the sound footing that God has never left himself without witness in the earth and that every religion has elements of real truth, he readily proceeded to the belief that no religion has it all. He dropped all thought of finality. Jesus Christ was indeed a great teacher alongside of Buddha and Mohammed, of Plato and Hegel and Gandhi—maybe a finer example of virtue than any of them, but in no way unique. The whole idea of a revealed religion dropped from him like a tattered garment.

Perhaps the true state of Bill's soul would not have become so transparent if he had not clung to his original intent of taking a pastorate. Here he delighted for a time those younger people who felt bound by conventional beliefs and practices. But even they soon began to press for answers or at least for some indication of what he had found that satisfied him. In vain Bill insisted that his role was simply to urge them on in their quest for answers and reasons. But man does not live by intellect alone; the final truth is found in leaps of faith, not in the weighings of the scales of logic. Bill by this time had no fast moorings to which he might point storm-tossed men and women even if he had thought it his place to do so. He told them he believed in God, but he gave them no clear picture of the kind of God who deserved to hold the allegiance of mature people. He tried to assure them that he felt life had meaning and purpose, but what the contents of those words might be he left vague. He believed, he said, in some form of immortality, though what real life he anticipated without resurrection from the dead he did not undertake to say. For him God was love in some sense of emotional concern, but he had no conviction of Jesus as the revealer of God's love in redemptive self-giving for men. He preached the gospel as an interesting point of view, but not as the living hope. He could argue for it but could not proclaim it.

Small wonder that Bill soon wears thin in any given situation and that he has wandered through several short pastorates in a few years. It is not narrowing but enlarging to hold sure faith in the uniqueness of one who is both savior and lord of life.

# Where Family Relations Enter In

## JOHN

Among all the problems and temptations of the minister, adjustment within his own family is often the most trying. I am not now thinking of the fight a young man so often goes through with his parents because he wants to enter the ministry and they had counted on his becoming a scientist, doctor, or lawyer. That is a trial of early youth that can be outrun as the man grows up and becomes disassociated from his boyhood home. But much more lasting is the problem of becoming reconciled to wife and children when they disapprove his choice, because he must live with them all the time. Most members of the church would be amazed if a seminary professor could divulge the confidences given him in this regard.

Often it is the case of a man who married before he felt the call to the ministry and whose wife is as surprised as anyone else at the change in his course of life. But even where she knew beforehand that her intended would serve through the church, she often has had no adequate idea of what that would mean to family life. She could not visualize her loved one as always in the limelight. She had not anticipated the incessant telephone calls day and night. She had not realized how closely the family life would be watched, especially if their ministry turned out to be in the smaller places. She could not forever guard the children against the so-called limitations of their status in the community. Sometimes her problem was accentuated by her upbringing; for example, she had come from an uneducated family or her own schooling had been poor or she had been used to more money than her husband could make. Occasionally such a minister's wife becomes a psychiatric case as a result of her failure to adjust to the unexpected.

The casual response of congregations to such conditions often is, Why don't seminaries give ministers' wives some training while they have them close by? Well, if we had unlimited scholarship funds, perhaps we could. But most seminary students' wives work during the day and they are too tired or find too many household chores to do in the evening, so that it is hard to get them into any classes. Many seminaries do indeed offer them evening instruction, at least one night a week, in such feminine basics as how to keep house, how to dress, how to raise children, or in the elements of subjects their husbands are studying such as a brief survey of the Bible, a simple summary of Christian theology and history, a discussion of church school materials, and the like. But response is often meager, and many wives who live far off campus and cannot get there need it most. They and their husbands drift further and further apart.

John was one of the fellows who suffered most in his seminary days from incompatibility. He had been a mountain boy himself and he had married in his late teens a mountain girl. True, they had gotten out of the hill country together and had gone to the college town, but she had clerked in a store while he had advanced in formal education. She had been raised in one of the sects, and she never could quite get reconciled to what she felt was the liberal attitude of the churches with which her husband was associated. Her family still held up to her at every chance the legalistic background of her youth: "You mustn't play cards, you mustn't dance, you mustn't wear lipstick—you mustn't, you mustn't." During John's first year in seminary she became quite upset emotionally. She withdrew from all possible association with her husband. She would not pray or read the Bible with him lest she become contaminated with some of the new ideas he was getting. And John was not the perfect handler of the situation. He had a quick temper and would sometimes let it loose on her most unmercifully, especially when she was accused (unjustly, as it turned out) of ogling other boys.

But John had one quality which others of the unadjusted often lack: tenacity. He held on, for he loved his young wife and he would not let her go. He won a graduate fellowship to a distant university and got her far removed from early moorings. He sought counsel and followed it. He had his reward, for she came at last to see his inherent worth. She put misgivings behind her, and together they found a useful ministry and raised a happy family. Would that the same sort of team ending could be written for others who have early pulled apart!

# MELVIN

Among the students whom he knows best the teacher sometimes finds himself ill at ease in trying to balance good and not so good. A natural liking for a fellow tends to close one's eyes to certain of his faults, yet in another sense opens a wider vision than would otherwise be available. For love is not blind, as it is supposed to be; it only sees deeper than any other quality of heart and therefore finds what others do not know is there.

It is good to feel that this represents my relationship with Melvin. I had known him before he came to the seminary; indeed because of his family's friendship with mine he was attracted our way. He never took advantage of this situation, nor did he curry favor. And as far as I know my own heart, I gave him no privileges beyond those I sought to bestow on all my students.

Yet social relationships have a way of spilling over into other phases of life. This is usually a good thing; its possible evils are only for those who are ready prey for the soft spots of life. So it was that Melvin often sought me out to discuss at length some idea that had germinated in class—my own or some other. In so doing he was careful not to seek my opinion of the professor or the student who had started him thinking along his new line, and this pleased me greatly. As always, I discussed ideas with him impersonally, seeking never to register any but a kind evaluation of his other friends.

But one day I woke up to the fact that he was imitating me. Now I have never learned to appreciate, even in the Apostle Paul, such an injunction as he wrote to his friends in Philippi, "Brethren, join in imitating me" (Phil. 3:17, R.S.V.). I understand well enough that he is urging his readers to follow him as he follows Christ, but his words still send shivers through me. So when I found that Melvin was aping even my gestures to a ridiculous extent, I became alarmed and sought a change.

Perhaps he saw my dilemma without fully understanding it. Perhaps he was even a bit hurt by my new attitude. Suffice it to say that when he began to date a certain girl in earnest, he said nothing about it to me. And when I found out that his parents and friends were alarmed by her unattractiveness and lack of friendliness, I suffered tortures of soul. But I held back from opening the matter with him; after all, a man's choice of a life partner is hardly subject even to the casual consideration of his friends. So I ground my teeth, thinking that here was a sterling fellow who was apt to be tied down for life with a less than suitable mate. Perhaps it was my anxiety that led me to fail to notice the waning of his interest in her, but after he had sidled up to some of us when his girlfriend was with him and gotten only a cold shoulder or a very indifferent conversation, he began to see the light. For a time he was quite depressed.

My surprise, then, sometime later was to learn from another source that Melvin had been going with another girl for some time. My delight was to have the privilege of being introduced to her and finding her one of the loveliest and most attractive young girls I had met in many a day. Melvin said nothing, nor did he come to see me, but some months afterward when he was away on a trip I received her parents' announcement of their engagement and from Melvin a postcard quoting the tenth verse from Paul's great thirteenth chapter of I Corinthians (k.j.v.): "But when that which is perfect is come, then that which is in part shall be done away." And I silently blessed the Lord for what had occurred and also for the grace that had been vouchsafed to me to keep my mouth shut and let things work themselves out. Close ties make waiting a very trying experience, but even the most delicate of circumstances is worked out for good when the Lord is dealing with a choice soul such as Melvin. Moreover it is quite true to fact that they "lived happily ever after," for she has been as fine a minister's wife as she was a match for Melvin. "Let patience have her perfect work" (James 1:4, k.j.v.).

# CALVIN

In my years in the service we have gone almost full circle in our thought of ministers' families. At one time they were scrutinized very closely. Especially during the prominence of the rural church, when the minister's wife was raked over the coals by the inquisitive sisters of the town and when the minister's children were often belabored for doing this or that which was all right for others to do, the tendency was to pity the poor unfortunates of the manse. As population became more centralized and the minister's job took on proportions of the administrator, the trained counselor, and the public citizen in addition to the long-recognized roles of preacher and pastor, it became popular to say, at least half audibly, How much better chance the Roman Catholic priest has to get his work done; he is without family cares.

But today, with the astonishing liberalizing of the Roman position, we are discovering how many priests there are who have felt their own lack from not knowing the family situation firsthand. As a matter of fact the Protestant minister has a tremendous advantage because of what a wife and children do for him to make him realistic in dealing with people and because of the opportunity they afford to set before the community an example of Christian home life. We know the ministers' wives who are misfits; we have heard all the tales of how badly some ministers' children turn out; but all joking aside, ministers' families are good families on the whole and from the manse comes a large proportion of the leaders in education, in the professions, and even in business. Who can minister more ably to others than he who knows what it means to gather his own around his fireside? And like all other fathers, he needs to guard the time that is sacred to them.

But there is the minister who is married and has no children. Unless he and his wife can identify with little children of other families, their marriage may be a stumbling block to the church. But there are some like Cal, who opened up the way in beautiful spirit. Cal was a delightful character and a fine husband. When it was determined beyond doubt that he and his wife could never have any children of their own, they began the process of adoption. To be sure, this procedure is always fraught with dangers. But Cal and his good helpmate have labored with such love and devotion that they have taken several youngsters from various kinds of homes and welded them into a Christian family that is outstanding in the community. Who knows the extra kind of heartache that has gone into this service? Who knows the deeper longings still unsatisfied? But they have made their adopted children truly their own. No one visiting them would ever guess that these children were not their flesh and blood. Together they have showed how to overcome many kinds of natural obstacles and be a unique blessing to home, church, and neighborhood.

Meanwhile, for the few single men in the ministry and for that larger number who, though married, have no children and who, for one reason or another, feel they cannot adopt any, be this borne deeply into the soul: Not only any minister but any adult who does not appreciate little children is a danger to any community. "Except ye . . . become as little children, ye shall not enter . . ." (Matt. 18:3, k.j.v.). And who can become as a little child unless he knows little children, can take their points of view, talk their language with them, see the world as they see it?

# Special Ministries

## DONALD

A high tribute to my students who have gone to serve overseas. Their name is not legion, yet their number has been respectably large. They have represented all sorts of preparation, all slants of theological thinking, many different fields of service. Some have been evangelists of the old order who have sought primarily to list converts to an outward expression of the Christian faith. Others have endeavored, without regard for statistical show, to win by their friendship and example men and women of other religions to higher motives for living, whether they have been willing to be listed as Christians or not. Some have been teachers whose steady work has borne fruit after much cultivation. Some have run hospitals; others have centered in agricultural improvements desperately needed by the people. One and all, they have been unselfish, giving themselves in time and strength with a completeness that has often made me wonder how they stood it and with a disregard for recognition that has put the rank and file of us to shame.

Of special interest is one who has financial means and who, having gone into overseas service through the church, has used his own money to buy land and start farm experiments with the people. In another case a student who knew little of machinery when he went out has learned to run a shop so that the boys in his school may have a source of income from salable products. In other instances, men whom I have had the privilege of teaching have themselves operated well-run schools, have prepared some of the local church for the ministry, often have translated into new dialects parts of the Bible and other literature. Some have produced educational materials suited to the people they served; some have pioneered in modern methods of communication, radio and television. One has even majored in dentistry while teaching his patients some of the biblical understandings he got in our classes.

Let Don serve as an example of many. He went to the foreign field with much of the older missionary complex. He was to give something to those who had nothing. There is enough of truth in this approach that we must never let it slip away; we do have a very distinctive message to proclaim. But it is not enough. Don soon found out that he must learn to work with those who were Christian leaders on their own field before he came. He must be a fraternal worker as well as a missionary. He rejoiced in the coming of the day when the church in the area he served could cut loose from the mother church in the U.S.A. and could establish its own government, direct its own mission, even send its own workers into other territories. He suffered the usual hardships of the implanted laborer: the need to fight native disease to which he had no natural immunity, the times of loneliness and discouragement with small returns, the difficulty of remaining fair in the midst of local politics and especially of revolution. He was sorely tempted, at least once, by an offer of promising Christian work in our own country, but after a furlough spent in praying and thinking it over, he and his good wife returned to take up their round once more. He is a living example of what so many who have served abroad have proved: the church does not operate mission work, but the church itself is mission.

I have never been able to agree with the position one often hears that every man who enters the ministry should consider first that the fields abroad have greater need than the field at home and that he therefore should show reason why he does not choose to go to some foreign land before he can conscientiously remain in the homeland. I believe, instead, not only that God calls a man into the ministry, but that he gives him a call within a call, that is, to a certain place and a specific kind of service. It is therefore for every man to determine where he believes the Lord would have him serve, and when he follows his conviction on that score, he is then a true missionary, whether or not he feels led to serve in the place of most obvious need. To be where one feels he is supposed to be and to render the kind of service he feels under God he is cut out to give—this is the crowning satisfaction of the Christian's life.

# TEACHERS A SCORE

I salute those whom I have taught who have themselves become teachers. Ten of them have entered the field of seminary teaching, several of these delighting me by joining the faculty as my younger colleagues. Others have been called to teach at the college level where they can influence young minds at an earlier stage in their development.

I am proud of all this group of ordained teachers who have been my pupils. Everyone of them has made good in the finest sense of that word. They have given the lie to the sneer one sometimes hears that ordained men leaving the pastorate for the teaching field are actually running from a hard life to something easier, from a leadership that puts them inevitably before the public to a position retired from all the spotlights. Nothing of the sort. The instructor of youth, especially one who teaches in the area of religion, is on the spot today as almost no other is. His utterances are closely watched. His beliefs are carefully weighed. If he adheres to the doctrines of the past, he is marked as irrelevant for his day. If he leads his pupils in fresh thinking and in action that ought to result from Christian premises, he is generally branded as dangerous to the faith. He can never bring up the rear guard of the church's forward march. He is constantly in the forefront of the battle. If he stumbles ever so little, he is pointed to as one who is unsafe for the trust that has been placed in his hands. If he guides with courage and brilliance, he is indeed appreciated by that ever growing segment of the church who respond to a more daring leadership, but he is feared by that larger group whose cherished beliefs or more highly cherished financial investments depend on keeping the status quo. All honor to my pupils who teach. Almost without exception they have really led the minds and hearts of their own pupils. They have been abreast of the issues of the day in both study and application. They have been not pedants, but pioneers.

The question is often asked whether a man should be placed in the teaching of religion, especially in a seminary, who has not had pastoral experience. My own answer is a decided No. The teacher needs the pastor's heart and the pastor's training so that he may truly be a pastor to those whom he instructs. For learning is a process not of amassing information but of discovering the meaning and use of truth. My students who have become teachers have first served a term in the give-and-take of the parish, and they have brought with them into their teaching relationships the heart and mind of the shepherd. Among them are those who are the cream of many years of labor by many of their own teachers. They have not been taken in by the vagaries of the day, but they have learned to use their skills in "rightly dividing the word of truth" (II Tim. 2:15, K.J.V.).

These teacher-pupils of mine have also become churchmen, almost without exception. They have not gone their individualistic ways and become, like some professors, leeches feeding on the body of Christ. But in their preaching as well as their teaching, in their writing as well as their counseling, in their active service in the church courts and their close relationship with people in many congregations, they have become humble day-by-day servants. The notion of some people that they do not know the church is a colossal blunder, for practically all of them have served again and again as moderators of particular parishes, as pulpit supplies of vacant churches, as counselors of parish officers, as visitors in homes and hospitals and business establishments. The instruction they give is enriched and kept realistic by these contacts with the living church. God be praised for those seminarians who teach!

# MILTON

Among the most doubtful results of the psychological tests which have been given to men entering the ministry are those that attempted to distinguish between masculine and feminine traits of personality. There was, for example, one test used for a long time which listed as tending dangerously toward femininity those who showed a distinct liking for music! Other tests have been almost as alarming at times and, in spite of the cautions added by those who prepare and administer them, have often frightened faculty needlessly about new men. For among those who have entered as question marks there have been several at least who have become noteworthy for their robust qualities.

Such a youth was Milton. Quiet and unassuming, loving not only music but flowers and art of all kinds, he was still a man through and through. Even the sweetness of his disposition was completely masculine. His thoughtfulness knew no bounds. He could anticipate the personal need of faculty member or fellow student and meet it with a dispatch and depth of understanding that both awed and delighted. Perhaps his variety of interests kept him alive to many of the concerns of others. His genuine Christian love made him a burden bearer who never appeared to be bearing burdens, only enjoying what he was doing for someone else. Yet he never lost himself in his helpfulness in such a way as to make his doing deeds of kindness an escape from his present duty. He was a high-ranking student, an apt director of a youth program in the church where his field experience lay, and he kept abreast of all his work.

I remember one bitter hour into which he entered with the deft touch of a Christian brother that has made me forever his debtor. It was a Saturday morning during the Second World War. I had just reached my office from the trying experience of driving my son to the induction center in response to his "greeting" from the President. I had held up with dogged determination in spite of a heart that was breaking, not only with the usual anguish of a parent who sees his child go off to war, but also with the fearful conviction that our being in that war was criminal. I was ready for an emotional letdown. Then came Milton's tap on my door. How he had discovered the situation I never learned, but he knew exactly what had been transpiring that morning. With a silent presence that betokened his good taste, with an empathy, both expressed and unexpressed, that touched the precise spot of need, he entered with me into my valley of the shadow and left me feeling that I had not only a son in the army but one right in my class.

It was most fitting that in the course of the years Milton should have become my assistant in discharging a certain duty that fell rather heavily upon me. Here again he was the quintessence of understanding, always anticipating the kind of aid I needed, never offering that which would have been out of order. He was the most complete combination of graciousness and strength, of modesty and forthrightness, that any man could ask for—one of the most truly ministering servants I have ever known. But the psychological tests had warned us that he was dangerous and would bear close watching! Well, I have watched, and the watching has been wonderful.


# DICK

Dick was one of our choice young men who wrestled with the question of military participation and who decided the issue in just the opposite way from that of the conscientious objectors. He went into the chaplaincy as a partial atonement for the fact that he did not have to serve in uniform because of being a student for the ministry.

He had no illusions about the chaplain's position. He knew that some men had entered it because they could get higher pay than they ever could expect in the pastorate. In fact, this was a leading reason that prompted him to enter; he wanted to show what an unselfish man could do as a spiritual leader in the muck and waste of war. He understood completely that some men in the chaplaincy were hamstrung by higher officers who would let them perform only trivial chores. He even knew that there were chaplains who did not care to do much more than they had to and who were seldom seen except in the PX drinking beer. But to Dick this was all the more incentive to show what a true military chaplain could be. He faced without flinching the answer to his candid question put to a representative of the Office of the Chief of Chaplains in Washington: Yes, he would have to be prepared to justify the war in which his men were fighting. He went through agonies of soul over this but still concluded that the chaplaincy was the call of God to him.

And he lived consistently within that call. He spent much time in this country and still more time abroad, largely on the high seas, often (as he put it) floating around at public expense, but always finding men to whom to minister, both those who were going through ordinary experiences of life and those who were in some crisis. As he wryly said one day, he had four times as may interviews on a ship going overseas as he did on one returning.

Dick has expressed himself as being ready to aid a movement, at any time the church is willing to lead it, to make all chaplains civilians so that they get no military rank or pay and especially so that they appear in the uniform of the church, not of the government. He agrees that all salaries of military chaplains should be paid by the church. He is the first to admit that the present situation is one of our grossest abuses of separation of church and state. But as he sardonically reminds us, "The church is by no means ready to bear the cost of supplying chaplains to all the armed forces, and I am not going to take up the cudgel which those who are not in my position should wield first." Perhaps, Dick, you may yet be the means of pointing us to something more consistent in our service to the men who are forced to be where many of us believe they should not be. For even if young men are compelled to go down into the deepest of earthly hells, the church of Jesus Christ should be the first to go with them.

# TODD

The art of communication has come front stage today. There was a time when seminary curricula touched this point only in relation to the preaching of sermons, the training of the minister's voice, and his effectiveness on the lecture platform. But the church is fast learning that the means of reaching people are now multiple. Radio broadcasts, television programs, revival of the use of drama in the church—these and many other approaches are emphasizing the variety of ways in which messages reach men. The appeal is to the eye as well as the ear, and the intended audience must participate as well as receive.

But glorious as these advances in communication media are, there is at least one grave danger in their use. Where the practitioner of homiletics was tempted to become engrossed only in the details of sermon preparation and speech, the man who uses the newer communication methods finds his tendency to overstress the technical compounded many times over. How shall this be avoided? I have watched rather closely several of my former students develop their mastery of this field, for both in the home church and abroad there are those who have specialized in this area. I take Todd as the example of the best handling of this work.

Todd did not start out as a mere technician. He was indeed skilled in the communicative arts when he came to seminary. But wishing to use them as a tool for spreading the gospel and not as an end in themselves, he realized that he must probe deeply into theology and all its related fields if he was to be outstanding in his chosen major. He did excellent work with me in biblical theology; his papers were carefully thought out, his reasoning clear. He likewise starred in other theological disciplines and in church history and Christian education. As a result, when he did graduate work in the arts of communication, he brought his theological discernment to bear upon these professional studies. He did not adopt just any religious play that came along; he carefully analyzed all of them and used only those he felt had a sound message. He did not debase the hours he was allowed in movie shows and telecasts to a display of scientific skill, but he focused all the fields of church concern in his choosing, auditing, and displaying of film and drama. More power to those in the future who become theologues with these new horizons!

# Contrasts

## MORRIS and HERSCHEL

How strange is the call of God! A teacher cannot foresee, as two men sit before him in class or in his office, how far apart their future paths may lie, how utterly different their types of ministry. They may be equally sincere and responsive, yet God may lead one into glorious public service with rich renown and the other to some hidden corner of the earth where he buries his whole life in the hearts of a few. Morris and Herschel used to pal around constantly in their student days, discussing life and its meaning, the church and its purpose. They were almost like brothers. How could one tell that Herschel would go to serve a huge church with a multiple staff and become a brilliant leader in ecclesiastical courts, while Morris would choose to be stuck away in the valleys of everyday farmers and woodsmen?

It was not that Morris had to stay there. While not so mentally agile as Herschel, he had many opportunities to leave his isolated kind of life and go to what the world would call richer pastures. But he has felt the urge to remain in the one place of service and to grow with the generations of one people. He has learned the little things of their daily existence as no transient minister could ever have done. He has enriched their poverty with certain farming knowledge and medical assistance, but never beyond a meager extent, for he has remained poor with them. He has brought some outside aid to the people in the form of nursing clinics and funds to build a church and school, but on the whole his is not a long story; it must be chronicled with "the short and simple annals of the poor." Yet his closeness to his people has produced in them an affection and loyalty beautiful to behold. He entered their part of the country in the days of meager communication; but even when better roads and television and bus service opened up the area to some extent, he continued to serve his people, as at the first, in homespun ways. He did not withdraw from the world; he read widely and visited all sorts of outside schools for refresher courses. But he always returned the same contented minister to the poverty of soil and board. And his family have never betrayed the least desire for any other kind of life.

What shall we say to these things? Is such a man a special kind of saint? Having given up the possibility of at least a measure of riches and having found life that was richer on that account, shall we say of him that he has followed the footsteps of the Master more closely than Herschel, for example— more closely indeed than any other of my pupils? Shall we recognize him as a Protestant Francis of Assisi?

Theoretically, at least, I think not. My experience with lives dedicated to the service of others through the gospel ministry has convinced me that such a man is equally a saint of God with any other who serves where and how he conscientiously believes God's will directs him. Herschel has felt just as strongly the divine guidance in his elegant cathedral-like church, ministering to those in the center of industrial planning who feast on the good things of life and have several huge homes and yachts and send their children to the finest private schools. He too is a Saint Francis in spirit. For the rich in this world have their heartaches and their sufferings no less deep down than do the poor. And Herschel has learned to know them and to heal their particular hurts. I have ministered with each of these men on his field of service and have noted how their people look up to them both and trust them.

Yet I must confess that this theoretical reasoning leaves me still somewhat uneasy in comparing the ministries of these two friends. It is not that I have the least doubt of the servanthood of either. Both men are humble; each is meeting a real need. Yet I have trouble getting past the feeling that Morris' ministry to the overlooked and the unimportant lies nearer the heart of Christ, that it is inherently a ministry of special purity of purpose, and that Herschel's service to the affluent, however noble in effort, will find no expression which can be quite so Christlike.

I devoutly wish that someone could remove this feeling from my mind. But is it not more nearly possible to cultivate the kingdom way of life among the disinherited than among the complicated machinery of the wielders of fortune? Even though the haves of Herschel's constituency include people of genuine spiritual depth and generosity, doesn't the very fact of their having so much make any ministry to them and through them less real than Morris' service to the have nots? "How hardly shall they that have riches enter into the kingdom of God!" (Mark 10:23, k.j.v.). And I believe that Herschel himself would join in adding, "It is easier for a camel to go through the eye of a needle" (Mark 10:25, k.j.v.).

# GLENN and MARTIN

All of my long experience of teaching in two institutions has been in the heart of America. I have seen our seaboard seminaries at work on both coasts and have admired them greatly. But there is something about being in the center of expanse—both north-south and east-west—that has given a sense of representativeness, brought enrichment from variety close at hand, and blended naturally into unity.

The most startling experience I encountered in such blending, perhaps the funniest single moment I can remember from all these years, has to do with the opening of seminary one mild September day. I happened to be on campus at the instant two new students arrived, one from northern North Dakota and the other from southern Mississippi. The former came in, bag and baggage, clad in a fur overcoat; the latter arrived in shirt-sleeves. They stopped and stared at each other as though each thought he was seeing a crazy man. Then I recalled from the morning weather report that a belated heat wave was sweeping the Gulf coast and that an early snowstorm had blanketed the extreme northland. I recovered from my immoderate merriment in time to go up to both of the fellows, learn their names, and introduce them to each other as upcoming classmates. The boy from North Dakota was as dignified and stiff as the cold blasts from which he had emerged. The lad from the Deep South was as warmly garrulous as the temperature of his home town might have suggested. I shook my head in hopeless wonder.

The story would not be so good if it ended there. But these two young men, so disparate in background, training, and disposition, became fast friends and remained for years after their school days intimate in correspondence. Truly the cross of Christ "has broken down the dividing wall of hostility" (Eph. 2:14, R.S.V.). Christian discipleship leaps all barriers. We are inspired to trust that not only the sectionalism of our own land may be destroyed, but that all across the world iron, bamboo, and gold curtains may come tumbling down. Berlin walls and barbed wire may be broken, and He shall make one all peoples of the earth to dwell together in its beauty. Of this let the seminary be the abiding symbol.

# HERBERT, JACK, LUKE

Administration is among the gifts which have been historically underrated in the ministry. I myself used to look down upon it as at least a lesser talent, for I knew I did not have it and I shied away from anyone who did. We all tend to admire the most those who excel in the arts of living that we think most vital and where we ourselves are eager to achieve.

But a number of men have gone through my classes, some of them good Bible students too, who have come out with a strong emphasis on the administrative side. A few of them, indeed, have been only good technicians, but a goodly number have developed a clear understanding of the principles involved in effective administrative work and have blessed the church thereby. There has long been a popular theory that the church suffers from too much administration, is organized from the top down, and is constructed somewhat like Ezekiel's wheels within wheels. Actually the church often suffers from too little organization, or at least from an organization that is not well thought out and is not theologically oriented to the basic purposes of the church.

Among those who have become men of renown in this field, some have worked hard enough to cripple their influence while still in their productive years; others have marred a good overall record by becoming hardened in their own mold. But there have been several who have towered above these mistakes. I think of three at almost the same moment, though they are miles apart in personality and method.

Herbert has always been an appealing fellow. I have been especially close to him and his family and have long admired and loved him. He has the true administrator's gift for persuading people. He is never dogmatic, everlastingly patient, always kind. Outwardly he does not seem to get a whole lot done in any given period. Yet over the years he has brought order out of comparative chaos in more than one situation.

Jack is a deep thinker. He sees administration in the light of the whole life of the church. He has the true ecumenical passion so essential in this day. He relates with consummate skill the problems of the local field to the worldwide enterprise of the kingdom. He has lifted the sights of more individuals and congregations than one could number. He has a facile pen, and his writing supports admirably his preaching and his planning. But primarily he is an administrator, gifted in sensing the unrealized need, remarkably capable in expressing that need so that men see and follow where he leads—a veritable Moses in the wilderness to the churches of his area.

Luke is still a different sort. Big and hearty, shunning the confines of the settled sections or the refinements of meticulous procedure, he roams vast areas and brings into some organizational form the scattered bits of the church. Luke is a molder of considerable skill, and he knows how to employ other men and keep them interested in the work.

These are three quite different types of workers, each of them excellent in his own way. The church needs more like them, and Paul was right when he listed administrators among those spiritually gifted in the body of Christ (1 Cor. 12:28, R.S.V.).

# Bruised Reeds

---

## DEAN

If only we could know the upsets that befall men at critical junctures, how much harshness might be removed from our judgments. Those who suffer most from such upsets and judgments often feel an embarrassed reluctance to reveal even to close friends the trial that has overtaken them at the most inopportune moment. Hard as it is to say, this reluctance may be due to a kind of inverted pride that shrinks from bothering others with its trouble lest it seem to be asking for preferential treatment. As over against those who cry out at every hurt, a person with such an attitude is, of course, to be desired.

Dean found the medium between these two in a way so manly I was really thrilled. I had always admired Dean. He had a strong, clean face and a noble bearing. He was not the best of students, but he always did well, especially on examinations. Hence I was totally unprepared for the paper I got from him at the end of the first semester of his senior year, a paper which he flunked flat. I thought first of having a talk with him before averaging it in with the rest of his work to make the lowest possible passing grade. But I instinctively felt that Dean was not the kind who would appreciate this, so I worked through to the end of my report and turned it in. Meantime Dean seemed to be avoiding me, and I was troubled about what to do.

After the second semester had gotten off to a full start, he sought me out. "Have you turned in the grades yet?" he asked. "Yes," I replied, "and I was very sorry . . ." But Dean held up his hand to stop me. "I know what you are going to say," he continued. "I know I failed that exam completely. And I did not want you to know why as long as there was any chance of my grade being affected by any sympathetic consideration. Now that it is decided, however, I'd like you to know the reason. Just as I was entering the room that morning to take your exam, the postman handed me a letter from my girl breaking our engagement. I simply couldn't think of a thing on the test. That's all."

No, that's not all, for there was a man. Small wonder that his sturdy, upstanding manhood has impressed itself wherever he has served in the ministry. The manhood of the Master lives in such men. Small wonder that what we might reverently chronicle in the words of a great preacher as "the expulsive power of a new affection" has since driven the hurt from his soul and has led him to a happy home and ministry.

# ALEX

Perhaps few people who have never been there can understand how lonely a student can get in a dormitory—not only a college student, but one who is at the more mature level of seminary work. This is true not only of the timid, somewhat childish type that sometimes reaches the graduate stage, but of the manly, up-and-coming fellow as well.

Alex had his idiosyncrasies, it is true. He could remain apparently passive for a long time in a controversial situation and then explode violently at the last. He was one of several students I have had who felt himself deeply in love with a girl, lost her to a fellow student, went to the wedding to congratulate the lucky bridegroom, and remained good friends with him ever after. For Alex was lovable, even when he got off-key, and delightful even when one differed sharply from him.

I would probably not have guessed what his loneliness meant to him had he remained silent after being in our home one evening. No doubt many another seminarian has felt like this but did not feel called upon to say anything about it. A teacher, like a pastor, often finds out only years afterward, and sometimes not directly at all, how some apparently insignificant relationship has remained for years a sweet memory in the life of the student. Alex said little about it that night and still less when I met him on campus during the following week. But sometime later we received from him a note which I have cherished both for its Christian fellowship and its gracious form of expression. In part Alex said,

> There is a certain type of loneliness that develops in a person who lives in a dorm, and I really can't say whether all the fellows have it—but I sure do. And the only answer to it is just being in a home. This is why that evening was especially meaningful to me and I am sure to all of us. Your warmth and kindness are so very much appreciated.

I do not quote these lines in the spirit of self-praise. Indeed they convict me as strongly as they comfort me, for while we have often befriended men away from home, all too often we have overlooked opportunities. This happenstance is set down in the prayerful hope that it may inspire others to get away from the distant, secondhand contacts with which we so often satisfy our consciences and find instead the joy that comes into life when we give, not of things, but of ourselves.

# DUNCAN

More often than one might think, a student can put a teacher to shame. Not very many of them would like to do it, but there are some few who can accomplish this with a healing grace. One of my most humiliating experiences sprang from Duncan's good spirit which stayed with him through my display of anger.

In fairness to myself let me say that I was justified in being angry. I had recommended Duncan for a high award, the winning of which was supposed to depend in part on his following the rules our department had laid down. Duncan won the award all right, but he did not play within the rules. Yet a benevolent committee gave him the benefit of the doubt because of attendant circumstances which they felt justified his lapses.

I was glad for him to win but could not share the feeling that his nonchalant attitude toward the manner of his triumph was excusable. This is not the place to argue whether he and the committee were fair or whether my sense of rectitude should have prevailed. In the nature of the case the circumstances have to be stated vaguely rather than be spelled out. The upshot of the matter was that I wrote rather strongly, emphasizing to Duncan how remiss I felt he had been and separating myself from any congratulatory tribute on his winning. After all, I had been responsible for seeing that he followed the prescribed way, and I was hurt that at the last others had excused him from what I had been instructed to lay on him as his duty. It was only after my anger and disappointment had cooled off a bit that I regretted not the contents, but the tone of my letter.

I had my reward. Duncan must have been reading the twelfth chapter of Romans, or else he was constitutionally inclined to live according to its principles. At any rate he knew how to heap coals of fire on my head. In reply to my rebuke, he wrote in the most conciliatory manner, "I am sorry that I have been a disappointment to you after all you have done to see me through. I want you to know how much I appreciate all you have been to me, including this dressing down you have given me. I shall continue to think as much of you as ever."

Of course no one could remain angry in the face of such a response. If Duncan had written wrathfully in reply, my pride might have remained in its upright position. As it was, it was duly humbled, humiliated indeed, and the fondness I had long felt for this one of my student friends flowed back as a pleasant stream through the channel of my thinking, leaving the debris of floodtide wrath to be dried up by the newly shining sun of forgiveness. Thank God for pupils who restore reason to perturbed professors!

# Closed Minds

## TOM

Tom was bright and he knew it. He also knew how he wanted to use that brightness, and he was extremely dogmatic. He could be very pleasant; meeting him for the first time, one felt he was quite thoughtful of others. But he had a violent temper; when it was aroused, you had to handle him with gloves.

Tom was exasperating in his insistence on small points. If he thought he was right (and he usually did), he could stand up a whole class for the remainder of the period or an entire church court for an hour at a time while he persisted with his peccadillo, threatening an appeal if he was ruled out of order. He loved controversy and he could sense the opportunity for it from afar. I have heard him argue for a quarter of an hour on the placement of a comma. Somehow he always succeeded in persuading enough of those around him that there was something important in what he was saying to insure him a hearing.

It is no wonder that Tom was an easy prey for sectarianism within the church. He became obsessed with the idea that the seventh day of the week was the time to worship publicly. He would not, however, leave his safe position within the pale of the "regular" church to join the Seventh-Day Adventists or some similar group, for there was this or that little point in which *they* were wrong. But he went to their meetings, mixed with their devotees, and drew some of them into his congregation where they became stirrers up of strife. He neglected even the most elementary pastoral calling for retreats and conferences on the seventh day.

Perhaps, Tom, you are only an exaggeration of what takes place in the lives of many ministers. It is not easy to separate the important from the trivial. Both in the formation of ideas and in the use of time, many men squander strength and talent on that which is really of little use. To learn with Matthew Arnold to see "life steadily and . . . whole" will free the spirit from the petty. But it takes balanced experience to gain the steady, wholesome look.

# CHARLES

Fundamentalism is a set of mind that flourishes in certain areas and at particular times but is ever lurking in the lives of churchmen. I know, for I tended strongly to be a fundamentalist in my youth. When I came out from under the spell of this attitude (for it is an attitude rather than a belief), I did what men so often do—took a violent dislike to anyone who was still entangled with it. So it was that I came to disdain Charles.

However, I will not charge myself with unwarranted prejudice against him from the outset. For Charles, like so many of his tribe, was sour and nasty and backbiting. Being sure that he had the truth, as all fundamentalists are, he came to class only to be confirmed in it. He appreciated courses that gave him new arguments for his already-established position. Steeped in one kettle of thought, he readily sat in judgment upon all those who were not in the same pot. He scared some of the more timid souls by predicting their dire fate if they did not believe. He had a sarcastic way of ending every argument with "That's what *you* think," as though a man had no right to think for himself—a belief which he probably held. All truth was revealed once for all, he knew the revelation, and that was it. On his term papers he would often write, "So and so says such and such, but I hold . . ." If he learned anything really new in seminary days, I failed to discover it.

Charles became an effective preacher—never at loss for a word, graceful in gesture, rather eloquent with compound sentences, logical if you admitted his premises. He could wave his Bible in his hand while standing outside the pulpit and in his dramatic delivery could quote chapter and verse for each assurance uttered. Without hesitation he answered every question that came his way and never owned to any uncertainty about anything from the Garden of Eden to the return of Christ. Nor was he content to propound his dogmatism alone. He hunted out the "unbelievers" in his congregation, the "unsaved" ministers in the courts of his church. He could smell heresy a mile off. He strove to compel uniformity in belief, if not in action. The notion that any saying of Jesus or Paul might be subject to more than one interpretation was terrifying to him. The possibility that the text might have been amended by the church at any point was rank unbelief. The person who sought a well-rounded theology, embracing more than the ancient systems had worked out, was anathema.

Charles, you still trouble me. Is it that down underneath you are afraid? What is the source of your rather slippery promises and your frequent failure to honor your word? Why do your ethics often seem as unorthodox to those who know you as their theology does to you? Why do you insinuate about other men without saying outright what you mean? It is not that I object to a great deal in your belief. I am conservative by nature, as most men are, and actually believe much that you do. But I never could believe it with all the Q.E.D.'s you put after it, nor could I condemn those who think otherwise, even on admittedly crucial matters. The Spirit gives to many men graces of understanding which I have never experienced. They may be badly wrong at points where we are right, but no man is saved by the preciseness of his theology any more than by his good deeds. Grace is still the one ground of salvation, even for the minister.

# DAN

The attitude of the fundamentalist is not limited to conservatives. The marked liberal may display it too.

Dan had been brought up in the narrowest confines of orthodoxy. He had a strong, unbending personality, and in his college days he had propounded his beliefs with terrific force and uncompromising defiance. His war experience shattered his straitlaced creed. Confronted with grossness and lewd actions, his self-assurance broke down for a time, and he wandered in the miasmas of doubt. When he recovered his composure, he found himself far out to the left in his thinking. Now the Bible seemed a very human book, its authors often mistaken men. His rigorous critical position led him to search for the inconsistencies he felt were abounding in the church's theology and practice. With avid devotion he followed the extreme leftists on the theological horizon.

But Dan was by no means kindly in his treatment of those as conservative as he once had been. He held up to constant ridicule those fellow students who clung to the traditional. Those who tried to argue for the reliability of the biblical text or the church's position he followed from one class to another with persistent denunciations. He was as brutal in his attacks on conservatives as ever he had been in baiting the wildest innovator. His fundamentalism had simply been transferred to his new liberal stance. He was still essentially the same in his spiritual outlook as he had been when he denounced those who did not accept every crossed *t* and dotted *i* of traditional belief. After his graduation he became the cross-examiner of every young man who sought ordination, and he urged the rejection of all those whose views were antiquated.

Beware, Dan! You were not born again; you simply changed sides in the hall of the ecclesiastical congress. You are still at heart the same Dan you were in your youth. Transformation of spirit, deep and searching, is your primary need. God grant that it may find you, for you are a man of ability and power.

# Rebels

---

## FRITZ

The effect of two World Wars upon seminary life and teaching runs deeper than any analysis has yet revealed. Especially is this true of the Second World War and its silencing of the liberal theology of the first quarter of this century. That liberalism never was as man centered as it has often been pictured. At least its most understanding proponents were as deeply rooted in the originality of God's grace as were the classical theologians of previous eras. Nevertheless it is true that there was an unwarranted optimism in the church when I began my ministry of teaching, an optimism based rather on theories of social evolution than on biblical faith in the transformation of man by divine power. That optimism had been abetted rather than lessened by the First World War when men still believed that by military victory we had made the world safe for democracy. It was perhaps inevitable that the disillusionment of the fast-living twenties and the economic recession of the thirties, plus the revival of Teutonic power with the advent of Hitler, should have occasioned violent reaction in theology. That a Barth could arise to do battle with the various European schools that stemmed from Hegel's religious philosophy was quite understandable and indeed welcome.

What came to be most unfortunate was the swing of the pendulum of belief violently to the other extreme and the development of a radical pessimism in the forties. This pessimism was not limited in its effect to schools of thought but found its exponents also in pastoral ministry.

An outstanding case among my former pupils was Fritz. He had devoured the writings of most of the modern philosophers during his prewar school days. After a happy pastorate or two he had gone as a chaplain in the latter days of conflict and had been involved in some of the American comeback in the war with Japan. He became completely disillusioned about human nature, and he was honest enough to face squarely the fact that, all propaganda aside, human nature was basically the same west as east. I asked him once if he had seen any of the terrible atrocities we read so much about. "Yes," he replied, "but all those I saw were perpetrated by Americans." By the time he had gotten to the front, our side was winning, and it is always the victor that has the opportunity and therefore the temptation to commit the atrocities. The Japanese had done it when they had the upper hand; now that we were winning, we were imitating them all the way.

Fritz returned to the pastorate soured and bitter. He continued to read, largely in the neo-orthodox theologians, but went even further than the most conservative. He became pessimistic about the church, about the salvability of human nature, even about the value of life itself. He sought refuge in fatalism. Yet he continued to preach and to pour forth a nearly hopeless message. For a time his shocking sense of futility seemed to cast a spell, but then it lost its hold and he left his people shuddering. He found some relief in the revival of liturgy in church worship, but it was long before he recovered any of the buoyant faith of his early ministry. That he did recover it at all is an exception to what happened to some others, for militarism takes its toll within the church's ministry as elsewhere. Thus the genuine grief it entails leads many men to forget the true basis of a Christian optimism: We "sorrow not, even as others which have no hope" (I Thess. 4:13, K.J.V.).

# TONY

Tony is boisterously modern. He was that way in college, and by the time he reached the seminary he had all the earmarks of the radical. As unkempt in personal appearance as he could possibly be, with slacks unpressed, shirttail flying in the wind, hair uncombed, beard long and scraggly—if he suggested any biblical character at all, it would probably be Elijah or John the Baptist.

But Tony certainly could not be called a voice crying in the wilderness. His was a voice heard calling most loudly through the halls of the seminary, stridently raised across the cafeteria counter during coffee break, continuing in long-winded harangues day and night around the campus. It was he who organized the students to participate in parades for various causes, who took part in more sit-in demonstrations than any other. It was he who gave more attention to organized colloquiums than to classroom subjects, who brought leftist enthusiasts from the city and surrounding areas to talk with small groups of students at late night bull sessions around the dormitories. It was he who induced some of them to meet with unchurched youth in beer joints out in town to discuss the burning issues of the day.

Tony had little use for the regular enterprises of the student body. He never appeared at their business meetings. He considered student get-togethers meaningless if there was no topic of burning interest to debate. He would not contribute to the student benevolence program on the ground that it was not truly benevolent, though through it the students each year brought someone from a foreign country to live and work in their midst. But he was most generous when any case of poverty or misfortune presented itself from the community round about. When he was to be found in student circles at all, it was always with the same gang. They ate together, sat together, often studied together, and anyone who craved an opportunity to talk with them had to show pretty decidedly his ground of interest in order to gain even a foothold in the closed corporation of their thinking.

What does Tony stand for? An evangelism of a new stripe? In a way. If we may strip off the ungainly exterior, we may find some very real religious sensitivity. And we have no right to condemn attitudes and actions, modes of dress and habits, simply because they are strange and we don't instinctively like them. On the other hand, one wonders why it is necessary for a man to get himself up in ungainly fashion just to be different. Does assuming a shocking stance really gain effective attention to the social need that desperately calls for men's concern? Or does it tend to make people feel that the cause is as outlandish as its advocate? If we must hit people over the head with our eccentricities in order to get them to see what we are neglecting today of the church's opportunity in the world, then blessed be the eccentricities. But it may turn out that people will be won to heartier support of unpopular reforms by those who take the pains to associate with them in ways that they can appreciate. It may yet become evident that some of those who are far out need to learn the art not only of communicating with the world which they so ardently seek to know, but also of communicating with the church!

# PERRY

Perry was an intellectual dynamo. He read everything he could lay his hands on that was at all modern in its outlook and that he had heard was abreast of the current situation. Among the post-Bultmannians he particularly delighted in the writings of Martin Buber. He followed Sartre's agnosticism nearly all the way. Men like Ogden and Macquarrie were his daily bread. When the death-of-God theologians came along, he went all out for their point of view. He could not sing loudly enough the praises of Cox and Altizer in particular.

He was very sure that at least the God of the Old Testament was dead and that we could well afford to bury him in favor of Jesus and his revelation of love. For him, as for others, this was not a form of denial of faith, but an avowal of a gospel with all the fervor of a new convert.

Perry became much intrigued with what he heard secretly around the campus about the faculty's overhauling of the curriculum. He proclaimed to everyone who would listen that seminary instruction started at the wrong place and majored in the wrong fields. The Bible, church history, and dogmatics— what were they? Same old stuff! Simply the records of what men thought and did in bygone ages, scarcely relevant to our day. Men entering the ministry should begin their studies with an effort to understand the secular city. If biblical subjects belonged in the curriculum at all, they should be reserved for the senior year after the student had made his acquaintance with vital matters at hand. Courses in Christian Education were wide of the mark of today's need; pastoral studies were concerned mostly with old-timers who were already in the church, not with outreach to modern man who couldn't understand the church and who felt no need of its gospel. Perry believed that a seminary campus off to itself was a huge mistake; every seminary should be part of a university complex, and this in turn should be in immediate contact with the philosopher on the street corner.

Perry's abilities and outspokenness often made him unpopular with fellow students and faculty. An able critic on campus readily begets jealousy. Secret admiration and open disdain are twin children of such jealousy. Perry would loudly flout the basic teachings of some of his professors in a day when "It was never so seen in Israel" (Matt. 9:33, k.j.v.).

Such a student is a stinging gadfly to any settled way of life. But, to employ a worthier figure, he is as leaven in the lump. He disturbs the unrisen batch of our thinking and so fulfills a good purpose. He may help us see the need for a number of changes. But I have one criticism to make of him. He flits from one school of thought to another almost inevitably. The last writer or speaker who is with him has him. He may yet learn that no man can serve even two masters and that he must determine eventually just who his one Lord is to be.

# EDGAR

Edgar was from the first as completely modern in his view of the ministry as a man could be. He was tremendously serious about everything. Like so many of the moderns in this torn and fearful age, he had very little fun about him. In the student body and in the churches with which he was associated, there were those who greatly enjoyed games and parties. Edgar looked down on such events as childish and would decline invitations to the point of being rude. He would not even participate in athletics—it was a waste of time.

Ed was quick to denounce anything that smacked of finality. He disdained to say with Paul, "I know, and am persuaded . . ." (Rom. 14:14, K.J.V.). He felt that most theology had buttressed its tenets with sweeping generalizations and that such theology could not be true in a great many given cases. He was a thoroughgoing existentialist in his philosophy of life; that which challenged him now in this particular situation was all that was important. Yet he had his own generalizations which he failed to see. He believed, for example, and quite rightly, that one of the greatest needs of the hour was a championing of Negro rights, and he would march endlessly and even join the sit-down strikes that protested the abuse of Negroes—in general. But when it came to working with a particular colored boy on a committee, Ed just couldn't do it; he would see that individual's shortcomings so strongly that he never could get along with him.

Ed was a great reader. Moreover, he would devour the points of view of authors who did not represent his slant, and though he followed them primarily to criticize, he was fair in most of his judgments. He would indicate his appreciation of the valuable insights in some books whose general tone he despised. He was by nature artistic, and artistry showed itself especially in the readable style of writing which he developed.

Ed was a determined champion of a newer viewpoint among seminary students: that men come to a school of theology to try out its offerings; that they align themselves with the church experimentally; that a candidate for the ministry need not consider himself pledged, certainly not for life; that the idea of call is something which should originate in a man's own experiential relationships, not in a sense of being laid hold on by God with a "Woe is unto me, if I preach not the gospel!" (I Cor. 9:16, K.J.V.). For this reason his contact with the church has been uncertain. At times he has served faithfully, but just when you feel he is ready to take on some major responsibilities, he is absent without explanation for some time.

Oh, for the Power in your life, Edgar, that can settle you and render you dependable. If you ever come to be one who can be counted on, the church will be richly blessed by your service and those outside the church will feel the impact of a Christian personality which, I am convinced, is real in its often hidden depths. You have become possessed with the idea of the secular city. Has it not always been secular? It seems to be largely in the twentieth century that you feel the church talks a language which the world cannot understand. You would demythologize not only the gospel, but the entire symbolism of Christian faith. If you can do that and find the bridge between your own faith and the lack of faith in those you would love to serve, you may yet bring forth new things from the storehouse of your ingenuity.

# RODGER

Rodg was the perpetual champion of academic freedom for both the student body and the faculty. He insisted that unity of belief and even oneness of testimony must be sacrificed to freedom of speech and action. He was never so happy as when doing battle for this cause, and he had an uncanny accuracy in putting his finger on the real ground of opposition that lay behind what critics said. Thus when any member of the seminary group was publicly attacked for questioning whether the virgin birth were literal history, or for critical analysis of the origin of the Gospels, he would emphatically declare that these charges were only smoke screens— that the people who made them were really trying to get at the active participation in social concerns or the increasing pacifism among faculty and students. In a time when national loyalty had become the most popular virtue of the day, he was scathing in his uncovering of facts to show that many who made a god out of patriotism were profiting financially from the shares they held in military industries. The bitterness with which he was often attacked and the continual effort that was made to silence him were the best proofs of the general truth of his viewpoint.

But Rodg had unfortunate inconsistencies. In his eagerness to see academic freedom carried over into worship, he organized a group of students to stay away from the daily chapel service. Eventually this group got to meeting in the student lounge at the time of chapel, and they would substitute for worship with their fellows free discussion of the newest radical thinking. Yet when any of these men was sent on a weekend to conduct worship services in some parish church, he would of course expect the members of that church to be present and would often be quite loud in criticism of their lack of support.

Rodg's attitude, noble as it was in many respects, soon raised some of the most important questions of the day. Is a man really fulfilling a *ministry* if he is only a social reformer? Does he actually testify effectively to Jesus Christ's unique revelation of the God of love? Is he himself truly loyal to the church that, in its best hours, has championed the liberty of thought and action that makes his stance possible? Though deeply Christian at heart, would not the complete independence of his way of living eventually lead him to forego any real religious motive? That he sees the point of some of these questions and wrestles with them within the context of Christian faith and life is at least a hopeful sign. Meanwhile his critics have much further to go than he in taking seriously the claims of the Master.


# NAT

Nat early became obsessed with the appeal of situation ethics. For him it is not enough that the church has always taught that any certain actions cannot be prescribed as always right or wrong. He was not convinced that Paul's heroic fight against legalism had gone far enough, nor that the church had ever taken seriously the degree of moral freedom which the Apostle had attained. Jesus' emphasis on the man rather than the institution, whether the Sabbath or property rights, was to Nat only a scratching of the surface. Was not any social rebellion justified at times?

Nat grew quite specific in his illustrations that he felt were timely. Why shouldn't it be good practice for a poor man who was smart at the trade to feather his nest by gambling? If other men were willing to run the risk of being victims, what was wrong with it? If the use of liquor leads to conviviality, why should it be looked down upon simply because the fellow in question might get too much and be unsafe in driving home from the party? If drugs and "trips" could be regulated so that they were pretty sure to bring fantastic pleasure, why not use them? If young people have to postpone marriage because of the expense of getting an education, what is really wrong with marital relations outside marriage itself? Nat even toyed with the idea advanced by some writers that the Bible does not actually decree against such sexual irregularities as fornication and homosexuality. In fact, though he was happily married himself and true to his wife, he would sometimes raise the question whether those who had no such happiness might not rightly find their satisfaction outside the marriage bond.

To be sure, students often discuss such questions in a merely theoretical vein and are not nearly so far out as they sound. But the trouble with Nat, as with most of his ilk, is that he fails to see the opposite error to legalism. He renders good service in emphasizing that rules cannot govern life, but he fails to distinguish between rules and standards. It was in vain that his friends in faculty and student body tried to get him to see that objective standards are not legalisms if there are reasons for them; they may reflect eternal principles. But Nat could not see, for example, that if love within the marriage bond has been found to be the only possible unselfish expression of sexual affection, then any violation of that bond is always wrong. Nat was the unfortunate victim of a half-truth that blinded his eyes to the full light of the gospel of self-sacrifice and true joy. It is not accidental that he has more and more often raised the question, Is life worth living? and that he sometimes describes himself as trying to find nothing better than a way out of this misery. For himself and for others he has fought bravely against despair in the deep heartache of much of modern living, but he has done it only with the spiritual tools which the noble-minded Stoic, such as Kim's *The Martyred,* finds available. That the gospel has a light which Stoicism never discovers is yet hidden from Nat.

# Martyrs
## of Today's Arena

---

## BYRON

Perhaps the saddest hours of my teaching ministry have been spent in the unrewarding effort of trying to help former students move from one community to another when their leadership in applying the gospel to the affairs of daily life has brought them to an impasse with the powerful proponents of traditionalism.

Byron was naturally attractive and had been greatly beloved in all his early ministry. I spent a weekend with him on the large field he had come to serve at a time when ten years of ministry had seemingly insured his acceptance with his people. They admired and followed him almost to a man. They sought his counsel at important points in their lives and in the critical junctures of the church, and they were invariably blessed by his obvious sincerity.

Then came the tests in quick succession: his cordial attitude toward union with a larger branch of his own denomination, his unwillingness to sanction or justify what he felt was a godless war, and especially his avowal of the Supreme Court's decision about education and race within the community. His championing of the rights and needs of the Negro seemed as natural as anything else he had done. I could not believe that his difference from the majority of his flock in these particulars would ever wean them from him. Yet I was too innocent of the selfish passions that fire men's hearts when their long-established way of life is threatened. It took only a few swift months to turn many of his closest friends into bitter enemies, demanding his very soul. The officers of his church called a congregational meeting during his vacation to slip through a demand for his resignation. Those who had been his intimates now walked in his neighborhood as though they hardly knew him. The pain was so great that he could not bear it long. If he had not known them so well, if they had not trusted him so implicitly with some of the closest secrets of their lives, if he had not baptized their children and married their youth and buried their aged for two decades, it might have been possible to live with such a situation for a little and then pull out without there being left on him a death-dealing mark. But to give them up in this rebellious mood was to him the stilling of the very pulse of life. His friends got him into another field, but he lived only a short time. He had lost a family of hundreds on the highway of life. He was as truly a martyr as any of those of another day who were burned at the stake or sawed in two.

People of God, if such I still may call you, how can you let your deep-set prejudice lead you to knife the best friend you ever had? I know that we must be sympathetic with the oppressor as well as with the oppressed, for he is the product of long-time failure to deal adequately with the most tormenting problems of life. But isn't the Christian spirit of such a fine texture that you can tame your madness and at least be kindly in your separation from one who loved you as no other ever did? The final test of God's sanctifying Spirit waits for the day when he accomplishes this in the lives of sinful men.

# PHILIP

One of the most frequent causes of heart searching among students of the twentieth century has been the attitude they should take toward the development of militarism in

America. Since I belong to that lost generation that has been swallowed up by two World Wars and several lesser ones, I can sympathize with the anguish of many young men and even with the extremes to which they sometimes go in their thinking and action. Many of these finally settle for the uneasy conclusion that mankind has not yet progressed beyond the point where the law of the jungle has to be invoked from time to time. On the other hand, more and more are becoming absolute pacifists who attempt to carry their theory of nonresistance into actual combat situations. For these the government has made a clearer and more cordial preparation than has the church by arranging constructive service which they may render in hospital units or in clerical positions or as willing guinea pigs testing out new forms of drugs. Even some candidates for the ministry have chosen to serve in these noncombatant relations rather than accept their automatic exemptions. The fact that the churches in the vicinity of their service have often turned a cold shoulder and even refused to let them sing in the choir is the shame of the modern household of God that fears unpopularity with the world.

But the more moderate conscientious objectors have often suffered still more deeply. They are those who are willing to serve in uniform but not to take combat training, those who do not denounce war in general but who feel deeply that we are in the wrong in some particular conflict, those who would not be conscientious objectors if our own nation were attacked but who do not see any international service performed by our running here and there throughout the world trying to put out brush fires of Nazism or Communism—those who, in a word, believe that our military more often get our country into trouble than defend it.

Such a one was Phil. Quiet and unassuming, he was nevertheless very determined in his stand. When told that he could not hold his field of student supply if he announced his unwillingness to support the current war, he did not back down as others of his persuasion did but spoke his piece and took the consequences. When faced later in his pastorate with the galling choice between losing his influence with large numbers of people or modifying his position, he clung to his convictions, expressed them clearly and without rancor, and trusted the long-term future to restore his influence. And his bet with the future has won out.

So be it, Phil. Your kind is needed in these days of situation ethics and few settled convictions. You will never line up a mass following behind you, but neither will you have to repent in anguish to set your heart aright.

# EDWIN

Edwin apparently was born with a persecution complex. There are Christians like that in all generations. If they had lived in the second century, they would probably have sought martyrdom; but since their milieu is the twentieth century, they revel in that more terrible disease of delighting to be misunderstood and misrepresented. Edwin simply could not help saying things that would encourage people to call him a heretic. He was drawn to conflict as a moth to the flame.

It was not that he actually had such strange or even different beliefs, but that he justly sought the right to put them in his own way. He spurned the repetition of catechisms. He firmly believed that he could put his ideas in better terms for his generation than any ancient verbiage could express them. Both his motive and his belief were sound, and to those in close brotherly relationships with him they were well within the bonds of Christian understanding. Yet he shied from baptizing any of them in traditional language as instinctively as a ten-year-old shies from the bathtub. He was commonly supposed, for example, to deny the deity of Christ, but I shall never forget the fine statement he gave me on his own accord one day when all that Christ meant to him came out in terms that included the divine. He simply would not repeat the phrases of Chalcedon in describing Jesus to men, but he had a modern expression of devotion worked out that would stand up to any of the great church councils.

Of course such a character is a paradox. On the one hand, he really longs for fellowship and understanding. On the other, he loves to go it alone, to fight the wars of the spirit against convention. It is no wonder that such a man often takes off in all directions at once like a modern Don Quixote. It is hard for him not to ridicule his fellows. What he himself does not do justice to, of course, is the fact that the church has as difficult a time placing his rebellious spirit in its fellowship as he has in finding his true relation. When his church court refused to ordain him after long and painful examination, there were those who felt they had turned away one of the best prospects for the ministry they had had in many a day. Yet the very men who voted against him were bewildered; they were not Ed's enemies as he thought them to be. Nor was he theirs, for he loved the church as well as his Lord devoutly. His zeal to be a reformer was genuine, but it was marred, as such zeal often is, by his overanxiety to criticize and destroy. The problem for both him and the church is that of communication, so much talked of today but actually as old as the hills.

Edwin finally found his place. Strangely enough, it was in the instruction of youth. Here he showed patience, moderation, and general good sense. He had a flair for writing and he could put ideas into succinct paragraphs that were thought provoking, clear, and winsome. He has gotten not a few people to reconsider what Christ may mean to them, though he shies from wooing any of them to the full-time ministry of the church. His life seems to me definitely worthwhile. Whether it would be stronger if he did not have the penchant for alienating people, only the Recording Angel knows.

# From the Personal Side

## MY OWN

I cannot close these brief recollections without a note of yet more personal gratitude. While my thanksgiving is for the great multitude of these my students, most of whom have so honored the ministry of our Lord, that thanks is intensified as I think that one of them has been mine in a very literal sense.

Perhaps any father is made glad when a son of his follows in his own profession. And if that son alters that profession for the better or emphasizes some part of it that he has not stressed, all the more gratitude is due from the father. After all, the son has his father's shoulders to stand upon and he should do better and go farther and refine more delicately the line of his father's work. That I had a son, who, like his father, felt the call to the ministry, and who, also like his father, felt the call within the call to become a teaching minister, has been the fulfilling of a dream. That he chose to go through the seminary where his father taught made possible the sharing of many joyous hours of thought and planning, of discussion and decision. That he did not choose the same position of the teaching ministry that he had sat under, but felt his part should be the training of men and women at the college level, adds assurance of the independence of his choice. That that ministry is being performed abroad instead of in our own land sounds the note of the worldwide love of God and the ecumenical nature of the church which I have rejoiced all along to have made clear.

It would not be fair, either to this son of mine or to the others who have been my pupils, if I attempted to analyze his mind and contribution as I have tried to do with them. For he is now identified, as they are not, and I could not possibly trust myself to do unprejudiced thinking in his case even as far as I hope I have been able to do with the others. Suffice it then to offer up my great joy that bone of my bone, flesh of my flesh, and product of my fireside is to be found among these who have been my students. For this a profound thanks to God.

Yet I would not stop here if I am to keep clear the full meaning of the church of Jesus Christ. For another son, raised in the same family and with the same parental love, has sought to express his faith in the life of the community through the church as a layman. A city manager in a situation where the political and the economic and the moral must be delicately interplayed, elder in his church with especial interest in the youth to whom he and his wife have given much time, he illustrates, as the son of many another father does, the true meaning of the laity—the *laos,* the people of God. In these days when we Protestants are emphasizing anew the priesthood of all believers, the fact that every member of the church is a minister in the name of Jesus Christ, I take special joy in saying that I have two ministers in my own family—one serving from the pew and the home, the other from the classroom and the pulpit. Thus may God's call to all our lives be a uniting of all his children in the one great Christian ministry of servant of the Lord. In such a consecration may all the sons and daughters of all of us live to his glory!

# THE
# MINISTRY
# OF TOMORROW

However fond the look back over the ministry of the past four or five decades, a sequel inevitably suggests itself: What shall we say of the future? We cannot turn the clock back or expect the rising ministry of the church to be just what the older illustrated. Many of those whose services have been remembered in these pages are already deep in the newer emphasis. Often these innovations are cause for rejoicing, for they are a marked improvement on some of the past. Frequently they give us pause and even fright, for they are, like most human movements, mixtures of good and bad or of good and not so good. These glimpses of the past and present mark for us what is attractive in the fresher paths that men are following and may be a warning of pitfalls into which we must not jauntily stumble.

For one thing, the ministry of these days is much franker than that of the earlier part of the century. It is more self-conscious, studies its own stance more ardently, believes (though often without saying so) that "The proper study of mankind is man." As a result, the newer ministry is not awed by authority; it is more tolerant of the spirit of rebellion, indeed often participates in that spirit. It has shaken itself free of many of the taboos that haunted ordained men of earlier days, the legalisms by which some of them were bound.

The ministry of tomorrow is coming of age in its evaluation

of high standards of education and clinical training. It under-
stands clearly that there is no premium on ignorance. It is
availing itself more and more of the values there are in sociology,
psychology, and philosophy, even of the atheistic variety. It is
rather easily syncretistic; it yearns to envelop in its preparation
and its service the humanistic outlook that has come to be so
popular.

As a corollary to this, it has become axiomatic that the
ordained man be an extrovert. The retiring, meditative type—
even though he brings forth choice morsels from his study—is
pretty well shunned by his parishioners. Dialogue with the
world has come largely to replace fear of the world or treatment
of the world as the enemy of faith. Bridging the gap between
men of the church and men of the street has been undertaken
in earnest. Although the church as a coffee shop on the boule-
vard for discussing the problems of living or the gathering place
for those who have retired into apartments may be only temporary gestures toward people who do not know their own needs,
the church is progressively moving out into the places where
modern man lives and works, and the ministry is more and
more leading the way in that move.

In all this there is much good; some of it we may hope and
pray will be permanent. In all of it there is also real danger
that must be faced if the church is to remain the church.

The ministry of the future needs to remember, for example,
that no matter how much dialogue between the church and
the world may be desirable, the mission of the church is also to
proclaim. We will never cease to have a message to declare.
Moreover, in light of the New Testament meaning, "the world,"
however friendly our approach to it, can never become a bosom
companion in our way of life. "The world" is still at enmity
with God. It is a marked improvement that the ministry approaches that fact with compassion rather than simple denun-
ciation, but it cannot ignore the fact itself without losing its
own soul. We are at once in the world and yet not of the
world. It is still true that "we have an altar" from which other
men "have no right to eat" (Heb. 13:10, R.S.V.). This is not a

return to advocating an attitude of withdrawal but a joyous appreciation of the distinctive fellowship of the church.

Again, it needs to become increasingly evident that we dare not worship the great god "relevancy." Though we are on the right track when we seek to speak in terms of our own day and in the language in which men talk with one another, there is a sense in which the gospel never has been relevant and never can be. It does not commend itself to most men as pertinent to their needs. Each of them must still be born again if he is to see in it what his deepest desires are craving. Transformation and not simply development still has priority of appeal.

The broad-ranging slogans of our newer theology give us much to think about, but they still do not mark out the main highways of our approach to men in the name of God's redemption. The passing chant of God is dead is still what it was to a Marcion of the second century, the mistaken fear that the God of the Old Testament was a cruel, judgmental deity who must pass from the religious scene. The passionate devotion to Jesus as the substitute for God falls flat before the realization that everywhere in the New Testament he is emphasized as the true revelation of what God all along has been—holy, righteous, and loving at one and the same time.

Likewise, the so-called new morality is not really new at all. It has always been true that practice of any given ethic depends in part on the circumstances surrounding its use. To be sure, the church has not always made this clear; absolutism has often attended the laying down of this and that rule of conduct, however petty, and it is to its credit that the more modern ministry has singled out this fact and held it up to scorn. But the danger signal is flashed when so many of those who preach situation ethics draw the absurd conclusion that there are no fixed standards of right and wrong. The ministry of the future must recover its balance, reasserting a definitive "Thus saith the Lord" without falling back into the clutches of a new legalism. It is always true under all circumstances that murder and theft and adultery are wrong, that the failure to use one's gifts or to minister to the needy is sin. The very toning down of the words that express the evil in man's nature —hate, selfishness, transgression, and the like—misses the mark of his dependence on God for real change of heart. Repentance must still be a right about-face.

The man or woman who goes into the ordained ministry of the church today is often at fault because of a loss of personal pride in his work, even as a frightful number of the artisans of the world have lost that pride in this computer age. The individual in church leadership often manifests too meager a devotional life, a lack of the sense of triumphant joy in the Lord that needs to characterize his appeal to men, especially in a period of doubt and frustration. He has frequently become secondhand in his attention to the traditional services of his calling. His sermons are sometimes short discourses on pallid themes. With the excuse of getting just the right word he frequently reads those sermons as prepared essays, often burying his head in his manuscript so that he can scarcely be followed. In all he says and does he gives so much attention to preciseness that he misses real communication with his hearers. He writes out and reads laboriously his public prayers. Much of the language of tradition he draws upon for those prayers, reveling in the thought that this binds the church of the present to that of the past and that the ancient liturgy has expressed man's needs in finer diction than he can muster. The newer minister is often, in fact, a puzzling paradox; he is a modern in thought and illustration, but in form and manner, in tone and verbiage, he belongs to the past. His prophetic proclamation of the gospel is either missing altogether or is reserved for a challenge to help right social wrongs. This last is excellent in itself, but it needs far deeper rootage in his own native worship of God than the minister may be likely to evidence. For we reverence the past, not when we copy its language or its methods slavishly, but when we adopt its glowing faith, when we strike out upon the path that is native to us as they did on that road that was new to them. In short, the ministry tends to turn to the past where it ought to manifest courage that is original and free, and to forget its moorings in sound theology and ethics while it loosely follows the trends of the times. Such contradictions in emphasis may readily spell defeat for the high purpose of the church.

If the ordained man of tomorrow really believes that the laity with whom he deals are as much a part of the ministry of the church as he is, he will set before them an example of eager and far-reaching faith. If he truly rejoices in the light of God that shines through all forms of religious response, he will indeed lay before his people the truth there is in Hinduism, Buddhism, Mohammedanism, and even American dilettantism, for he will be forthright in saying that God has not left himself without witness anywhere in the earth. He will, like the author of the Epistle to the Hebrews, see other men's faith at its best, not at its worst. But he will also, like that same eloquent writer, magnify the uniqueness of Jesus Christ who is always better than any person or any service that can be produced by any other faith. His ecumenism must result, not in a loss of ardor for that which is peculiarly ours, but in a more gracious and outreaching declaration of his own fervency of faith.

Still another tendency that must be carefully watched in the ordained leadership of the church of today grows out of a welcome change in the layman's attitude toward the minister's needs. The habit of allowing the pastor and his family to live on as little as possible is passing rapidly from most church procedures. So long as it is the members of the church who sense the need for an overhauling of practice at this point, the accomplishments are likely to be worthy. But all too often the more modern seminary graduate starts out with his own strong emphasis on what he is worth or what he is sure he needs. He is encouraged by the church agencies to say just what income he will require. Right here is raised the specter of a former day when a man who was placed in a parish was thought of as having received a benefice, settled in a living. With all the compassion we have learned to feel for the underpaid minister of our earlier American scene, and with all due gladness for the efforts that have been put forth in recent years to bring him up to a decent standard of financial independence and social competence, there is an even more urgent need that he be kept conscious of his high motive. Of all professional men he especially must live above the atmosphere of those who strike for their rights. His must be the supreme illustration of a life of giving rather than of getting. He is the follower of a Master who said simply, even bluntly, "I am among you as one who serves" (Luke 22:27, R.S.V.).